HEINEMANN POETR

Selected Po

DH Lawrence

Selected by James Reeves

Edited by Andrew Whittle

Series Editor: Andrew Whittle

Heineman Educational,
a division of Heinemann Publishers (Oxford) Ltd
Halley Court, Jordan Hil, Oxford OX2 8EJ

OXFORD LONDON EDINBURGH
MADRID ATHENS BOLOGNA PARIS
MELBOURNE SYDNEY AUCKLAND SINGAPORE TOKYO
IBADAN NAIROBI HARARE GABORONE PORTSMOUTH NH (USA)

Selected Poems of DH Lawrence first published in Poetry Bookshelf 1951.
This edition first published 1995.
The publishers and Series Editor are indebted to James Reeves for his work as
Founding Editor of the orginal Poetry Bookshelf series.

10 9 8 7 6 5 4 3 2 1
99 98 97 96 95

A catalogue record for this book is available from the British Library on request.
ISBN 0 435 15080 4

Cover design by The Point

Text design by Roger Davies

Typeset by Books Unlimited (Nottm)

Printed by Clays Ltd, St Ives plc

CONTENTS

From *Birds, Beasts and Flowers*

From *Pansies*

INTRODUCTION

D H Lawrence was a novelist, a poet, a play-wright, a literary critic and a painter. He was one of the most important and controversial literary figures and innovators in the development of early twentieth-century English literature.

Lawrence's short life (1885–1930) spanned a period of great social and political change. Lawrence's father was a miner but his mother encouraged her son's education. His novels and poems are often at least partly autobiographical and reflect his attempts to come to terms with his own upbringing and relationships, as well as his view of people and society. Lawrence was in part a moralist who believed that people were in danger of losing touch with nature and with their own natural impulses. In his novels he describes nature, human impulses and relationships with great immediacy and vitality, and his frank writing about sex meant that some of his novels were declared obscene and suppressed. However, Lawrence refused to compromise in his writing. He saw himself as pushing forward the boundaries of convention and form in both his novels and his poetry. (You will find more about Lawrence, his work, life and times in Critical Approaches, pages 158 to 167.)

The poems

D H Lawrence wrote poetry all his adult life. Eight collections were published in his lifetime:

Love Poems and Others (1913)
Amores (1916)
Look! We Have Come Through! (1917)
New Poems (1918)
Bay: A Book of Poems (1919)
Tortoises (1921)
Birds, Beasts and Flowers (1923)
Pansies (1929)

In the last years of his life Lawrence set about editing his poetry and in 1928 published two volumes of his *Collected Poems* entitled *Rhyming Poems* and *Unrhyming Poems*. After his death, two more volumes of his poetry were published: *Nettles* (1930) and *Last Poems* (1932).

The poems in this selection follow the order and versions in the *Collected Poems* (apart from *Beyond the Rockies*). This order was chosen by Lawrence because, as he wrote in his preface to the *Collected Poems*, 'they make up a biography of an emotional and inner life'.

Notes, approaches and explorations

In this edition you will find glossary notes on pages opposite the text for ease of reference, together with points to help you think about the poems and develop your own personal responses.

In the **Critical Approaches** section you will find information about Lawrence's life, writing, poetic form, themes and ideas. The **Explorations and Essays** section contains activities to help you explore the ideas discussed in **Critical Approaches** and questions for extended writing. Finally, you will find **Writing an Essay about Poetry** and **A note from a Chief Examiner** useful in helping you prepare for extended coursework assignments and examinations.

From *Love Poems, Amores* and *New Poems*

Dog-Tired

This was first written in about 1908 when Lawrence was studying for his teaching diploma, and was first published in **Love Poems**. Like many others, this poem was altered for the **Collected Poems**.

7 *harebells* – a plant with slender stems and bell-shaped blue flowers found in open grassland (not to be confused with the bluebell, which is found in woods).

8 *vetch* – a climbing plant with blue or purple flowers and a bean-like fruit.

What are the feelings and mood conveyed in this poem?

From *Love Poems, Amores* and *New Poems*

Dog-Tired

If she would come to me here
    Now the sunken swaths
    Are glittering paths
To the sun, and the swallows cut clear
5 Into the setting sun! if she came to me here!

If she would come to me now,
Before the last-mown harebells are dead;
While that vetch-clump still burns red!
Before all the bats have dropped from the bough
10 To cool in the night; if she came to me now!

The horses are untackled, the chattering machine
Is still at last. If she would come
We could gather up the dry hay from
The hill-brow, and lie quite still, till the green
15 Sky ceased to quiver, and lost its active sheen.

I should like to drop
On the hay, with my head on her knee,
And lie dead still, while she
Breathed quiet above me; and the crop
20 Of stars grew silently.

I should like to lie still
As if I was dead; but feeling
Her hand go stealing
Over my face and my head, until
25 This ache was shed.

Discord in Childhood

This autobiographical poem from **Amores** describes the often brutal relationship between the poet's parents. In chapter 4 of **Sons and Lovers**, Lawrence also describes the shrieking 'almost demonic noise' of the tree outside the house where Paul Morel, alias Lawrence, wakes up to hear the boom of his father's drunken shouts and the sharp replies of his mother.

7   *thong* – a whiplash or a leather whip.

How does this poem create a link between the sound of the trees and the voices inside the house? (Look at the patterns which repeat in both verses.)

Cherry Robbers

An early study of relationships between men and women, this poem is also from **Love Poems**. The poem mirrors a passage in chapter 11 of **Sons and Lovers**. In three short stanzas it summons up a real or imagined incident containing promise of sexual adventure but also possible disappointment.

7   *throstles* – a poetic or dialect name for song-thrushes.
7   *robberlings* – petty thieves, a local dialect word.

What is the effect of juxtaposing the contrasting 'red' images with the lure of the girl?

Discord in Childhood

Outside the house an ash-tree hung its terrible whips,
And at night when the wind rose, the lash of the tree
Shrieked and slashed the wind, as a ship's
Weird rigging in a storm shrieks hideously.

5   Within the house two voices arose, a slender lash
Whistling she-delirious rage, and the dreadful sound
Of a male thong booming and bruising, until it had drowned
The other voice in a silence of blood, 'neath the noise of the ash.

Cherry Robbers

Under the long dark boughs, like jewels red
In the hair of an Eastern girl
Hang strings of crimson cherries, as if had bled
Blood-drops beneath each curl.

5   Under the glistening cherries, with folded wings
Three dead birds lie:
Pale-breasted throstles and a blackbird, robberlings
Stained with red dye.

Against the haystack a girl stands laughing at me,
10   Cherries hung round her ears.
Offers me her scarlet fruit: I will see
If she has any tears.

Virgin Youth

An earlier and very different version of this poem was printed in **Amores**.

16 *Homunculus* – a miniature man or kind of midget. Lawrence clearly revels in this latinate (from the Latin) word.

23 *iconoclast* – a person who destroys sacred or religious images.

What is your response to this poem's directness? Is it over-explicit? Is it an apt description of a young man's emotion and experience?

An earlier draft of this poem was called The Body Awake. *How does the title suit the poem? Why do you think Lawrence changed it?*

Virgin Youth

    Now and again
    The life that looks through my eyes
    And quivers in words through my mouth,
    And behaves like the rest of men,
5   Slips away, so I gasp in surprise.

    And then
    My unknown breasts begin
    To wake, and down the thin
    Ripples below the breast an urgent
10   Rhythm starts, and my silent and slumberous belly
    In one moment rouses insurgent.

    My soft, slumbering belly,
    Quivering awake with one impulse and one will,
    Then willy nilly
15   A lower me gets up and greets me;
    Homunculus stirs from his roots, and strives until,
    Risen up, he beats me.

    He stands, and I tremble before him.
    —Who then art thou?—
20   He is wordless, but sultry and vast,
    And I can't deplore him.
    —Who art thou? What hast
    Thou to do with me, thou lustrous one, iconoclast?—

    How beautiful he is! without sound,
25   Without eyes, without hands;
    Yet, flame of the living ground
    He stands, the column of fire by night.
    And he knows from the depths; he quite
    Alone understands.

47-9   *I am helplessly bound...virginity* – a reference to Andromeda, who in
       Greek myth was chained to a rock as a sacrifice to a sea-monster
       which was ravaging her father's kingdom. She was rescued by Perseus.

30 Quite alone, he alone
   Understands and knows.
   Lustrously sure, unknown
   Out of nowhere he rose.

   I tremble in his shadow, as he burns
35 For the dark goal.
   He stands like a lighthouse, night churns
   Round his base, his dark light rolls
   Into darkness, and darkly returns.

   Is he calling, the lone one? Is his deep
40 Silence full of summons?
   Is he moving invisibly? Does his steep
   Curve sweep towards a woman's?

   Traveller, column of fire,
   It is vain.
45 The glow of thy full desire
   Becomes pain.

   Dark, ruddy pillar, forgive me! I
   Am helplessly bound
   To the rock of virginity. Thy
50 Strange voice has no sound.

   We cry in the wilderness. Forgive me, I
   Would so gladly lie
   In the womanly valley, and ply
   Thy twofold dance.

55 Thou dark one, thou proud, curved beauty! I
   Would worship thee, letting my buttocks prance.
   But the hosts of men and with one voice deny
   Me the chance.

Monologue of a Mother

This poem was originally published in **Poetry** magazine as A Mother of Sons, then in revised form in **Amores** and finally altered for **Collected Poems**. It expresses the emotional torment felt by a mother when her son leaves home.

11 *chaunting* – an archaic (old or obsolete) alternative form of *chanting*.

12 *weird* – an archaic word meaning fate or destiny, or (as here) a magic spell or charm.

22 *chafes* – becomes irritated or impatient.

What is happening to the mother in this poem? Why does her son seem 'strange' to her?

How does the mother's mood and train of thought change at the end of the poem? How does she view the rest of her life?

They have taken the gates from the hinges
60 And built up the way. I salute thee
But to deflower thee. Thy tower impinges
On nothingness. Pardon me!

Monologue of a Mother

This is the last of all, then, this is the last!
I must fold my hands, and turn my face to the fire,
And watch my dead days fusing together in dross,
Shape after shape, and scene after scene of my past
5 Clotting to one dead mass in the sinking fire
Where ash on the dying coals grows swiftly, like heavy moss.

Strange he is, my son, for whom I have waited like a lover;
Strange to me, like a captive in a foreign country, haunting
The confines, gazing out beyond, where the winds go free;
10 White and gaunt, with wistful eyes that hover
Always on the distance, as if his soul were chaunting
A monotonous weird of departure away from me.

Like a thin white bird blown out of the northern seas,
Like a bird from the far north blown with a broken wing
15 Into our sooty garden, he drags and beats
Along the fence perpetually, seeking release
From me, from the hand of my love which creeps up, needing
His happiness, whilst he in displeasure retreats.

I must look away from him, for my faded eyes
20 Like a cringing dog at his heels offend him now,
Like a toothless hound pursuing him with my will;
Till he chafes at my crouching persistence, and a sharp spark flies
In my soul from under the sudden frown of his brow
As he blenches and turns away, and my heart stands still.

The Little Town at Evening

This poem was first published in 1919, in **Poetry** magazine, in **The Monthly Chapbook** and then in **Bay**, although it was written much earlier. Like *Last Hours* and *End of Another Home Holiday*, the poem explores human emotions from an autobiographical viewpoint.

In your view, is the female personification of the church effective?

How does the mood and tone of the poem change between the first stanza and the last two?

25 This is the last, it will not be any more.
All my life I have borne the burden of myself,
All the long years of sitting in my husband's house;
Never have I said to myself as he closed the door:
"Now I am caught! You are hopelessly lost, O Self!
30 You are frightened with joy, my heart, like a frightened mouse."

Three times have I offered myself, three times rejected.
It will not be any more. No more, my son, my son!—
Never to know the glad freedom of obedience, since long ago
The angel of childhood kissed me and went! I expected
35 This last one to claim me;—and now, my son, O my son,
I must sit alone and wait, and never know
The loss of myself, till death comes, who cannot fail.

Death, in whose service is nothing of gladness, takes me;
For the lips and the eyes of God are behind a veil.
40 And the thought of the lipless voice of the Father shakes me
With dread, and fills my heart with the tears of desire,
And my heart rebels with anguish, as night draws nigher.

The Little Town at Evening

The chime of the bells, and the church clock striking eight
Solemnly and distinctly cries down the babel of children still
playing in the hay.
The church draws nearer upon us, gentle and great
5 In shadow, covering us up with her grey.

Like drowsy creatures, the houses fall asleep
Under the fleece of shadow, as in between
Tall and dark the church moves, anxious to keep
Their sleeping, cover them soft unseen.

Last Hours

Like *End of Another Home Holiday*, this poem evokes the poet's feelings as he faces a return to Croydon some time in 1906.

5   *crocketed* – a crocket is a projecting carved leaf or flower placed at regular intervals on the sloping sides of spires, pinnacles and gables in Gothic architecture, giving them a knobbly, bristling appearance.

7   *sorrel* – a plant of the dock family, which bears a spike of red flowers, followed by reddish-brown seeds, at the top of a central stem.

7   *cresset* – a light made by burning a wick in a hollow container of oil or fat.

20   *clomb* – the archaic past tense of *climb*.

21   *insouciant* – carefree or lighthearted.

What is the poet musing over as he waits?

Does the regular rhyme in the poem trivialize the feelings he is describing?

10 Hardly a murmur comes from the sleeping brood;
    I wish the church had covered me up with the rest
    In the home-place. Why is it she should exclude
    Me so distinctly from sleeping the sleep I'd love best?

Last Hours

The cool of an oak's unchequered shade
Falls on me as I lie in deep grass
Which rushes upward, blade beyond blade.
While higher the darting grass-flowers pass
5   Piercing the blue with their crocketed spires
And waving flags, and the ragged fires
Of the sorrel's cresset—a green, brave town
Vegetable, new in renown.

Over the tree's edge, as over a mountain
10 Surges the white of the moon,
A cloud comes up like the surge of a fountain,
Pressing round and low at first, but soon
Heaving and piling a round white dome.
How lovely it is to be at home
15 Like an insect in the grass
Letting life pass!

There's a scent of clover crept through my hair
From the full resource of some purple dome
Where that lumbering bee, who can hardly bear
20 His burden above me, never has clomb.
But not even the scent of insouciant flowers
Makes pause the hours.

Weeknight Service

Although this was first published in **Amores** it really belongs to a group containing *End of Another Home Holiday, The Little Town at Evening* and *Last Hours*.

6   *orator* – a public speaker, specifically one who makes speeches designed to persuade or inflame an audience.

Down the valley roars a townward train.
I hear it through the grass
25 Dragging the links of my shortening chain
Southwards, alas!

Weeknight Service

The five old bells
Are hurrying and stridently calling,
Insisting, protesting
They are right, yet clamorously falling
5 Into gabbling confusion, without resting,
Like spattering shouts of an orator endlessly dropping .
From the tower on the town, but endlessly, never stopping.

The silver moon
That somebody has spun so high
10 To settle the question, heads or tails? has caught
In the net of the night's balloon,
And sits with a smooth, bland smile up there in the sky
Serenely smiling at naught,
Unless the little star that keeps her company
15 Makes tittering jests at the bells' obscenity;
As if *he* knew aught!

While patient Night
Sits indifferent, hugged in her rags;
She neither knows nor cares
20 Why the old church bellows and brags;
The noise distresses her ears, and tears
At her tattered silence, as she crouches and covers her face
Bent, if we did but know it, on a weary and bitter grimace.

29   *chaff* – tease, banter with (slang)

32   *cenotaph* – a funerary monument (literally 'empty tomb') with no-one
     buried beneath it. The best-known example is the Cenotaph in
     Whitehall, London, which commemorates the dead of World Wars I
     and II.

What is the overall mood of the poem?

What associations could the moon, stars and Night carry in this poem?

*Do you think the church is benign in this poem? Compare the poet's attitude
to this church with the one in* The Little Town at Evening.

Letter from Town: On a Grey Morning in March

Both this poem and *Letter from Town: The Almond Tree* appeared in **New
Poems**, but were first published in **New Poetry** and had originally been
written to Jessie Chambers in about 1910–11.

3   *aglance* – to one side.

15   *peewits* – birds (also known as lapwings).

The wise old trees
25 Drop their leaves with a faint, sharp hiss of contempt;
A car at the end of the street goes by with a laugh.
As by degrees
The damned bells cease, and we are exempt,
And the stars can chaff
30 The cool high moon at their ease; while the droning church
Is peopled with shadows and wailing, and last ghosts lurch
Towards its cenotaph.

Letter from Town: On a Grey Morning in March

The clouds are pushing in grey reluctance slowly northward to you,
While north of them all, at the farthest ends, stands one bright-
bosomed, aglance
With fire as it guards the wild north-coasts, red-fire seas running
5 through
The rocks where ravens flying to windward melt as a well-shot lance.

You should be out by the orchard, where violets secretly darken
the earth,
Or there in the woods of the twilight, with northern wind-flowers
10 shaken astir.
Think of me here in the library, trying and trying a song that is worth
Tears and swords to my heart, arrows no armour will turn or deter.

You tell me the lambs have come, they lie like daises white in
the grass
15 Of the dark-green hills; new calves in shed; peewits turn after
the plough—

22   *sough* – a sighing or murmuring sound (to rhyme with 'how' or 'bough').

Does the imagery in the poem imply any worries Lawrence might have or tensions between himself and Jessie Chambers?

Identify the chivalric or Arthurian imagery, the rural and the urban imagery. What values do they each reflect? What is your response to the juxtaposition of these images in the poem?

Letter from Town: The Almond Tree

What do the images in stanza 3 evoke for you? Why do you think Lawrence chose to shift the focus of his thoughts and the location at this point in the poem?

In the last stanza Lawrence portrays quickly-changing images of the woman in the poem. If the woman is Jessie, how do you think Lawrence feels about their relationship?

20 It is well for you. For me the navvies work in the road where I pass
    And I want to smite in anger the barren rock of each waterless brow.

    Like the sough of a wind that is caught up high in the mesh of the
    budding trees,
25 A sudden car goes sweeping past, and I strain my soul to hear
    The voice of the furtive triumphant engine as it rushes past like a
    breeze,
    To hear on its mocking triumphance unwitting the after-echo of fear.

Letter from Town: The Almond-Tree

    You promised to send me some violets. Did you forget?
    White ones and blue ones from under the orchard hedge?
    Sweet dark purple, and white ones mixed for a pledge
    Of our early love that hardly has opened yet.

5   Here there's an almond-tree—you have never seen
    Such a one in the north—it flowers on the street, and I stand
    Every day by the fence to look up at the flowers that expand
    At rest in the blue, and wonder at what they mean.

    Under the almond-tree, the happy lands
10 Provence, Japan, and Italy repose;
    And passing feet are chatter and clapping of those
    Who play around us, country girls clapping their hands.

    You, my love, the foremost, in a flowered gown,
    All your unbearable tenderness, you with the laughter
15 Startled upon your eyes now so wide with hereafter,
    You with loose hands of abandonment hanging down.

End of Another Home Holiday

Originally written in 1910–11 but published in **Love Poems**, this poem returns to the sentiments of *Last Hours* and shares certain themes with *Piano* (see page 49).

3 *phlox* – a white-flowered, scented garden plant, originally from North America.

End of Another Home Holiday

When shall I see the half-moon sink again
Behind the black sycamore at the end of the garden?
When will the scent of the dim white phlox
Creep up the wall to me, and in at my open window?

5 Why is it, the long, slow stroke of the midnight bell
  (Will it never finish the twelve?)
Falls again and again on my heart with a heavy reproach?
The moon-mist is over the village, out of the mist speaks the bell,
And all the little roofs of the village bow low, pitiful, beseeching
10 resigned.
—Speak, you my home! what is it I don't do well?

Ah home, suddenly I love you
As I hear the sharp clean trot of a pony down the road,
Succeeding sharp little sounds dropping into silence
15 Clear upon the long-drawn hoarseness of a train across the valley

    . . . .

The light has gone out, from under my mother's door.
 That she should love me so!—
 She, so lonely, greying now!
 And I leaving her,
20 Bent on my pursuits!

 Love is the great Asker.
 The sun and the rain do not ask the secret
 Of the time when the grain struggles down in the dark.
 The moon walks her lonely way without anguish,
25 Because no one grieves over her departure.

44 *heifer* – a young cow.

56 *cauterise* – to seal or destroy body tissue by burning.

Forever, ever by my shoulder pitiful love will linger,
Crouching as little houses crouch under the mist when I turn.
Forever, out of the mist, the church lifts up a reproachful finger,
Pointing my eyes in wretched defiance where love hides her face
30   to mourn.

Oh! but the rain creeps down to wet the grain
That struggles alone in the dark,
And asking nothing, patiently steals back again!
The moon sets forth o' nights
35   To walk the lonely, dusky heights
Serenely, with steps unswerving;
Pursued by no sigh of bereavement,
No tears of love unnerving
Her constant tread:
40   While ever at my side,
Frail and sad, with grey, bowed head,
The beggar-woman, the yearning-eyed
Inexorable love goes lagging.

The wild young heifer, glancing distraught,
45   With a strange new knocking of life at her side
Runs seeking a loneliness.
The little grain draws down the earth, to hide
Nay, even the slumberous egg, as it labours under the shell
Patiently to divide and self-divide,
50   Asks to be hidden, and wishes nothing to tell.

But when I draw the scanty cloak of silence over my eyes
Piteous love comes peering under the hood;
Touches the clasp with trembling fingers, and tries
To put her ears to the painful sob of my blood;
55   While her tears soak through to my breast,
Where they burn and cauterise.

.   .   .   .

58 *corncrake* – a once-common field and meadow bird with a repetitive and rasping call.

60 *plaintive* – expressing melancholy, sorrow and sadness.

> What are the concerns and forces buffeting the poet in the poem?

> Do you consider that 'Love is the great Asker' (line 21) reveals the central theme of the poem? If so, how?

Baby Running Barefoot

This poem, published in one version in **Amores** and originally written in 1909, is one of a group written about the baby, Hilda Mary, the daughter of Mr and Mrs Jones with whom Lawrence was lodging while teaching in Croydon.

6 *winsome* – charming or attractive.

13 *syringa* – another name for the lilac flower.

14 *peony* – a large shrub with red, white, yellow or pink flowers.

> What images and associations does 'a wind-shadow' convey to you?

> How do the syntax and enjambment in the poem imitate the flutter of the child as she moves around the garden?

> Pick out some words and phrases that express the extended metaphor in this poem.

The moon lies back and reddens.
In the valley a corncrake calls
Monotonously,
60   With a plaintive, unalterable voice, that deadens
My confident activity;
With a hoarse, insistent request that falls
Unweariedly, unweariedly,
Asking something more of me,
65   Yet more of me.

Baby Running Barefoot

When the white feet of the baby beat across the grass
The little white feet nod like white flowers in a wind,
They poise and run like puffs of wind that pass
Over water where the weeds are thinned.

5   And the sight of their white playing in the grass
Is winsome as a robin's song, so fluttering;
Or like two butterflies that settle on a glass
Cup for a moment, soft little wing-beats uttering.

And I wish that the baby would tack across here to me
10   Like a wind-shadow running on a pond, so she could stand
With two little bare white feet upon my knee
And I could feel her feet in either hand

Cool as syringa buds in morning hours,
Or firm and silken as young peony flowers.

Aware

Whilst in Croydon, Lawrence was friendly with another teacher called Helen Corke. He also kept up a relationship with Louie Burrows, a friend from his pupil-teacher days. After the death of his mother and his rejection of Jessie, he was engaged to Louie from 1910–12. Published in **Love Poems**, *Aware* was written after Jessie visited London in 1909.

1   *ruddy* – glowing, highly-coloured or reddish.

2   *shift* – a simple, usually sleeveless, dress.

> What words or phrases describing the moon are metaphorically applied to the woman?

A White Blossom

This poem was also published in **Love Poems**.

2   *bower* – a shady or leafy shelter.

> What does the moon symbolize in this poem?

> Contrast the symbolism of the moon in this poem with the symbolism of the moon in *Aware*.

Corot

As a teacher in Croydon, Lawrence had the opportunity to visit the great London art galleries. Jean-Baptiste Corot was a nineteenth-century French landscape painter whose work Lawrence tried to copy. Here Lawrence recalls a painting and then broods on his own thoughts about life and Time. This poem was also published in **Love Poems**.

Aware

Slowly the moon is rising out of the ruddy haze,
Divesting herself of her golden shift, and so
Emerging white and exquisite; and I in amaze
See in the sky before me, a woman I did not know
5 I loved, but there she goes, and her beauty hurts my heart;
I follow her down the night, begging her not to depart.

A White Blossom

A tiny moon as small and white as a single jasmine flower
Leans all alone above my window, on night's wintry bower,
Liquid as lime-tree blossom, soft as brilliant water or rain
She shines, the first white love of my youth, passionless and in vain.

Corot

The trees rise taller and taller, lifted
On a subtle rush of cool grey flame
That issuing out of the east has sifted
The spirit from each leaf's frame.

5 For the trailing, leisurely rapture of life
Drifts dimly forward, easily hidden
By bright leaves uttered aloud; and strife
Of shapes by a hard wind ridden.

9 *plasm* – the yellowish liquid part of the blood in which the cells are suspended.

9 *limpid* – clear or transparent (also calm and peaceful).

9 *pellucid* – perfectly transparent or translucent.

11 *athwart* – across, transversely.

16 *gossamer's* – fine cobwebs, often seen on foliage or floating in the air.

16 *rime* – frost.

19 *sheaves* – plural of *sheaf*; bundles of cut cereal stalks (such as wheat) or any similar bundle.

28 *the wheel* – probably the chariot-wheel of 'advancing Time'.

What phrases suggest that Lawrence is thinking of a painting? What sort of setting and view is he describing?

What atmosphere do the recurring images of the trees bring to the poem?

Which phrases or words emphasize the imagery of life and blood in the poem?

What do the poet's thoughts turn to in the latter half of the poem? What is its overall mood?

The grey, plasm-limpid, pellucid advance
10 Of the luminous purpose of Life shines out
Where lofty trees athwart-stream chance
　　To shake flakes of its shadow about.

The subtle, steady rush of the whole
Grey foam-mist of advancing Time
15 As it silently sweeps to its somewhere, its goal,
　　Is seen in the gossamer's rime.

Is heard in the windless whisper of leaves,
In the silent labours of men in the field,
In the downward-dropping of flimsy sheaves
20 　　Of cloud the rain-skies yield.

In the tapping haste of a fallen leaf,
In the flapping of red-roof smoke, and the small
Footstepping tap of men beneath
　　Dim trees so huge and tall.

25 For what can all sharp-rimmed substance but catch
In a backward ripple, the wave-length, reveal
For a moment the mighty direction, snatch
　　A spark beneath the wheel!

Since Life sweeps whirling, dim and vast,
30 Creating the channelled vein of man
And leaf for its passage; a shadow cast
　　And gone before we can scan.

Ah listen, for silence is not lonely!
Imitate the magnificent trees
35 That speak no word of their rapture, but only
　　Breathe largely the luminous breeze.

After the Opera

This poem from **Bay** stems, like *Corot*, from Lawrence's many cultural visits to London. It is also an early example of his social comment.

What is the poet's mood in this poem?
Is he mocking the theatre-going crowd?
Does his mood change at the end of the poem?

Lawrence is tentatively exploring free verse in this poem. What effect do the different line lengths have?

Morning Work

This light-hearted piece from **Love Poems** records a glimpse of manual activity. The symmetry of the poem enhances Lawrence's observation of a magical moment.

6   *crystalline* – like, or containing, crystals; glittering.

7   *cerulean* – sky-blue.

What phrases and images carry magical or fairytale associations?

What words and sounds suggest the light-hearted approach the workers have to their toil?

After the Opera

Down the stone stairs
Girls with their large eyes wide with tragedy
Lift looks of shocked and momentous emotion up at me.
And I smile.

5 Ladies
Stepping like birds with their bright and pointed feet
Peer anxiously forth, as if for a boat to carry them out of the
    wreckage;
And among the wreck of the theatre crowd
10 I stand and smile.
They take tragedy so becomingly;
Which pleases me.

But when I meet the weary eyes
The reddened, aching eyes of the bar-man with thin arms,
15 I am glad to go back to where I came from.

Morning Work

A gang of labourers on the piled wet timber
That shines blood-red beside the railway siding
Seem to be making out of the blue of the morning
Something faery and fine, the shuttles sliding.

5 The red-gold spools of their hands and their faces swinging
Hither and thither across the high crystalline frame
Of day: trolls at the cave of ringing cerulean mining
And laughing with labour, living their work like a game.

Last Lesson of the Afternoon

This poem, *A Snowy Day in School* and other school poems were published as a sequence called *The Schoolmaster* in **Love Poems** in 1912, after Lawrence had left teaching. The poems express his love/hate approach to teaching, his anger with the antics of the pupils and the futility of learning for no reason.

4   *quarry* – a person or animal being hunted; anything pursued. Lawrence has deliberately left the meaning ambiguous.

15   *dross* – worthless: literally, the scum from the top of molten metal.

20   *abyss* – a chasm or hole of immeasurable depth.

23   *all my aunt* – an obsolete colloquialism meaning 'irrelevant, nonsense'. The nearest modern equivalent might be 'a load of rubbish'.

How successful do you think the hunting metaphor in the first stanza is?

Last Lesson of the Afternoon

When will the bell ring, and end this weariness?
How long have they tugged the leash, and strained apart,
My pack of unruly hounds! I cannot start
Them again on a quarry of knowledge they hate to hunt,
5   I can haul them and urge them no more.

No longer now can I endure the brunt
Of the books that lie out on the desks; a full threescore
Of several insults of blotted pages, and scrawl
Of slovenly work that they have offered me.
10   I am sick, and what on earth is the good of it all?
What good to them or me, I cannot see!

           So, shall I take
My last dear fuel of life to heap on my soul
And kindle my will to a flame that shall consume
15   Their dross of indifference; and take the toll
Of their insults in punishment?—I will not!—

I will not waste my soul and my strength for this.
What do I care for all that they do amiss!
What is the point of this teaching of mine, and of this
20   Learning of theirs? It all goes down the same abyss.

What does it matter to me, if they can write
A description of a dog, or if they can't?
What is the point? To us both, it is all my aunt!
And yet I'm supposed to care, with all my might.

25   I do not, and will not; they won't and they don't; and that's all!
I shall keep my strength for myself; they can keep theirs as well.
Why should we beat our heads against the wall
Of each other? I shall sit and wait for the bell.

A Snowy Day in School

This poem is another in the *Schoolmaster* sequence, written between 1910 and 1911 and published in 1912. The poet's sense of tedium and frustration is vividly evoked.

4 *pattered* – gabbled, repeated without understanding.

A Snowy Day in School

All the long school-hours, round the irregular hum of the class
Have pressed immeasurable spaces of hoarse silence
Muffling my mind, as snow muffles the sounds that pass
Down the soiled street. We have pattered the lessons ceaselessly—

5 But the faces of the boys, in the brooding, yellow light
Have been for me like a dazed constellation of stars,
Like half-blown flowers dimly shaking at the night,
Like half-seen froth on an ebbing shore in the moon.

Out of each face, strange, dark beams that disquiet;
10 In the open depths of each flower, dark, restless drops;
Twin-bubbling challenge and mystery, in the foam's whispering riot.
—How can I answer the challenge of so many eyes?

The thick snow is crumpled on the roof, it plunges down
15 Awfully!—Must I call back a hundred eyes?—A voice
Falters a statement about an abstract noun—
What was my question?—My God, must I break this hoarse

Silence that rustles beyond the stars?—There!—
I have startled a hundred eyes, and now I must look
20 Them an answer back; it is more than I can bear.

The snow descends as if the slow sky shook
In flakes of shadow down; while through the gap
Between the schools sweeps one black rook.

In the playground, a shaggy snowball stands huge and still
25 With fair flakes lighting down on it. Beyond, the town
Is lost in this shadowed silence the skies distil.

29 *wrangle* – argue, struggle or contend.

29 *rood* – an archaic word meaning crucifix or cross. Christ was forced to carry the cross on which he was crucified. Lawrence may be alluding to the expression 'to bear one's cross', which means to endure hardship or misfortune; he may, on the other hand, simply be comparing the day metaphorically with slow crucifixion for both himself and his pupils.

What symbolism and associations are suggested by the imagery of the snow and stars? How does Lawrence reinforce his meaning?

Does Lawrence seem more determined to change his life than he did in Last Lesson of the Afternoon, *or is he more resigned to his situation?*

A Winter's Tale

This little poem was first seen in **The Egoist** magazine in April 1914 and then in **Amores**. The form of the poem is quite regular compared with the seemingly casual approach of *A Snowy Day in School*.

How does the rhythm of the poem suggest the reluctant trudge of the poet to this possibly painful meeting?

What is the tone of the poem and what are Lawrence's thoughts in the last line?

Sorrow

This poem appears in **Amores** but was first published in **Poetry** in 1914, under the name *Weariness*. Both *Sorrow* and *Brooding Grief* are deeply autobiographical poems written while Lawrence's mother was dying.

Why does the poet repeat his questioning in the first stanza of Sorrow?

Look at the way lines rhyme across stanzas as well as within them. How does this reflect the poet's train of thought?

And all things are in silence, they can brood
Alone within the dim and hoarse silence.
Only I and the class must wrangle; this work is a bitter rood!

A Winter's Tale

Yesterday the fields were only grey with scattered snow,
And now the longest grass-leaves hardly emerge;
Yet her deep footsteps mark the snow, and go
On towards the pines at the hill's white verge.

5 I cannot see her, since the mist's pale scarf
Obscures the dark wood and the dull orange sky;
But she's waiting, I know, impatient and cold, half
Sobs struggling into her frosty sigh.

Why does she come so promptly, when she must know
10 She's only the nearer to the inevitable farewell?
The hill is steep, on the snow my steps are slow—
Why does she come, when she knows what I have to tell?

Sorrow

Why does the thin grey strand
Floating up from the forgotten
Cigarette between my fingers,
Why does it trouble me?

5 Ah, you will understand;
When I carried my mother downstairs,
A few times only, at the beginning
Of her soft-foot malady,

Brooding Grief

This poem was first published in 1915 in an anthology entitled **Some Imagist Poets**. The Imagists, a group of English and American poets, organized before and during the First World War, included Ezra Pound. They felt that Lawrence's poetic experiments, see also *On the Balcony*, were near to their aim of producing poems with phrases or short lines of rhythm rather than a regular rhythmic pattern.

5   *brindled* – streaked or patched with a dark colour.

Is the theme in this poem the same as Sorrow? How is it investigated here?

Snap-Dragon

First published in **The English Review** in June 1912, this poem also appeared in the collection **Georgian Poetry** in the same year and then in **Amores**. The Georgian Poets (including Walter de la Mare, Rupert Brooke and Siegfried Sassoon) wrote predominantly nostalgic and lyrical personal poems about the beauty of rural and natural subjects, and did not experiment to any great extent with poetic form. It is easy to see how some of Lawrence's earlier pieces might have matched some of the ideals of the Georgians, but he rejected their values as too tame, escapist and bourgeois.

The version here was Lawrence's final reworking and was included in **Collected Poems**. This sensual poem, which has been described by the poet James Reeves as 'a sort of psychological short story in verse', explores the poet's awakening sexuality.

7   *mien* – a person's appearance or expression.

I should find, for a reprimand
10   To my gaiety, a few long grey hairs
On the breast of my coat; and one by one
I watched them float up the dark chimney.

Brooding Grief

A yellow leaf, from the darkness
Hops like a frog before me;
Why should I start and stand still?

I was watching the woman that bore me
5   Stretched in the brindled darkness
Of the sick-room, rigid with will
To die: and the quick leaf tore me
Back to this rainy swill
Of leaves and lamps and the city street mingled before me.

Snap-Dragon

She made me follow to her garden, where
The mellow sunlight stood as in a cup
Between the old grey walls; I did not dare
To raise my face, I did not dare look up,
5   Lest her bright eyes like sparrows should fly in
My windows of discovery, and shrill "Sin!"

So with a downcast mien and laughing voice
I followed, followed the swing of her white dress
That rocked in a lilt along; I watched the poise
10   Of her feet as they flew for a space, then paused to press
The grass deep down with the royal burden of her;
And gladly I'd offered my breast to the tread of her.

30 *Grail* – an archaic word for a bowl. The Holy Grail was the bowl or
    chalice used by Christ at the Last Supper and was sought after by King
    Arthur's knights as a symbol of spiritual regeneration.

32 *amethyst* – a purple or violet quartz gem.

*Look carefully at the rhyme scheme and the length of verses in this poem.
How does the structure mirror what is happening to the poet?*

"I like to see," she said, and she crouched her down,
She sunk into my sight like a settling bird;
15 And her bosom couched in the confines of her gown
Like heavy birds at rest there, softly stirred
By her measured breaths: "I like to see," said she,
"The snap-dragon put out his tongue at me."

She laughed, she reached her hand out to the flower,
20 Closing its crimson throat. My own throat in her power
Strangled, my heart swelled up so full
As if it would burst its wine-skin in my throat,
Choke me in my own crimson. I watched her pull
The gorge of the gaping flower, till the blood did float

25   Over my eyes, and I was blind—
          Her large brown hand stretched over
          The windows of my mind;
          And there in the dark I did discover
          Things I was out to find:

30 My Grail, a brown bowl twined
   With swollen veins that met in the wrist,
   Under whose brown the amethyst
   I longed to taste! I longed to turn
   My heart's red measure in her cup;
35 I longed to feel my hot blood burn
   With the amethyst in her cup.

   Then suddenly she looked up,
   And I was blind in a tawny-gold day,
   Till she took her eyes away.

40 So she came down from above
   And emptied my heart of love.
   So I held my heart aloft
   To the cuckoo that hung like a dove,
   And she settled soft.

46   *reiver* – a northern dialect word meaning robber or bandit.

52   *mutable* – liable to change.

Why do you think Lawrence placed one stanza in italics?

45 It seemed that I and the morning world
Were pressed cup-shape to take this reiver
Bird who was weary to have furled
Her wings in us,
As we were weary to receive her.

50 *This bird, this rich,*
Sumptuous central grain;
This mutable witch,
This one refrain,
This laugh in the fight,
55 *This clot of night,*
This field of delight.

She spoke, and I closed my eyes
To shut hallucinations out.
I echoed with surprise
60 Hearing my mere lips shout
The answer they did devise.

Again I saw a brown bird hover
Over the flowers at my feet;
I felt a brown bird hover
65 Over my heart, and sweet
Its shadow lay on my heart.
I thought I saw on the clover
A brown bee pulling apart
The closed flesh of the clover
70 And burrowing in its heart.

She moved her hand, and again
I felt the brown bird cover
My heart; and then
The bird came down on my heart,
75 As on a nest the rover
Cuckoo comes, and shoves over

83   *dint* – a dent.

91   *mordant* – sharp, biting
92   *cleaved* – split by a blow from an axe or sword.

105   *deeps* – depths.

                The brim each careful part
                Of love, takes possession, and settles her down,
                With her wings and her feathers to drown
80   The nest in a heart of love.

            She turned her flushed face to me for the glint
            Of a moment.—"See," she laughed, "if you also
            Can make them yawn!"—I put my hand to the dint
            In the flower's throat, and the flower gaped wide with woe.
85   She watched, she went of a sudden intensely still,
            She watched my hand, to see what it would fulfil.

            I pressed the wretched, throttled flower between
            My fingers, till its head lay back, its fangs
            Poised at her. Like a weapon my hand was white and keen,
90   And I held the choked flower-serpent in its pangs
            Of mordant anguish, till she ceased to laugh,
            Until her pride's flag, smitten, cleaved down to the staff.

            She hid her face, she murmured between her lips
            The low word "Don't!"—I let the flower fall,
95   But held my hand afloat towards the slips
            Of blossom she fingered, and my fingers all
            Put forth to her: she did not move, nor I,
            For my hand like a snake watched hers, that could not fly.

            Then I laughed in the dark of my heart, I did exult
100   Like a sudden chuckling of music. I bade her eyes
            Meet mine, I opened her helpless eyes to consult
            Their fear, their shame, their joy that underlies
            Defeat in such a battle. In the dark of her eyes
            My heart was fierce to make her laughter rise.

105   Till her dark deeps shook with convulsive thrills, and the dark
            Of her spirit wavered like watered thrilled with light:

Firelight and Nightfall

This contemplative poem comes from **Amores** but was first published in **Poetry** in December 1913. There is a sense of grief and death in this poem.

3 *sheaves* – literally, bundles of reaped corn.

6 *hyacinth* – a flower, also a colour ranging from purplish-blue to violet. This is also another name for jacinth, a reddish-brown mineral.

8 *diapered* – a diaper is a woven design consisting of diamonds. As a verb, it means to decorate in such a pattern.

8 *chaunting* – an archaic form of *chanting*.

And my heart leaped up in longing to plunge its stark
Fervour within the pool of her twilight,
Within her spacious soul, to find delight.

110 And I do not care, though the large hands of revenge
Shall get my throat at last, shall get it soon,
If the joy that they are lifted to avenge
Have risen red on my night as a harvest moon,
Which even death can only put out for me;
115 And death, I know, is better than not-to-be.

Firelight and Nightfall

The darkness steals the forms of all the queens,
But oh, the palms of his two black hands are red
Inflamed with binding up the sheaves of the dead
Hours that were once all glory and all queens.

5 And I remember still the sunny hours
Of queens in hyacinth and skies of gold,
And morning singing where the woods are scrolled
And diapered above the chaunting flowers.

Here lamps are white like snowdrops in the grass:
10 The town is like a churchyard, all so still
And grey now night is here; nor will
Another torn red sunset come to pass.

A Passing-Bell

A passing bell is the one that is tolled at funerals.

What is the purpose of the lines in italic? Should they be read as part of the poem? Do they add any extra meaning to the poem?

What events or emotions does this poem evoke?

Piano

This autobiographical poem, rewritten in about 1911 first appears in **New Poems** and recalls the intense relationship between the poet and his mother. The woman singing to the accompaniment of the piano evokes conflicting and nostalgic memories of the poet's childhood and his mother. Each stanza develops related ideas as the dual images are sketched out.

2 *vista* – a view, especially one seen through a long, narrow passage or opening.

A Passing-Bell

Mournfully to and fro, to and fro the trees are waving,
  What did you say, my dear?
The rain-bruised leaves are suddenly shaken, as a child
Asleep still shakes in the clutch of a sob—
5 *Yes, my love, I hear.*

One lonely bell, one only, the storm-tossed afternoon is braving,
  Why not let it ring?
The roses lean down when they hear it, the tender, mild
Flowers of the bleeding-heart fall to the throb—
10 *'Tis a little thing!*

A wet bird walks on the lawn, call to the boy to come and look,
  Yes, it is over now.
Call to him out of the silence, call him to see
The starling shaking its head as it walks in the grass—
15 *Ah, who knows how?*

He cannot see it, I can never show it him, how it shook
  Don't disturb it, darling!—
Its head as it walked: I can never call him to me,
Never, he *is* not, whatever shall come to pass.
20 *No, look at the wet starling!*

Piano

Softly, in the dusk, a woman is singing to me;
Taking me back down the vista of years, till I see
A child sitting under the piano, in the boom of the tingling strings
5 And pressing the small, poised feet of a mother who smiles as she
  sings.

11 *appassionato* – a musical term for intense and passionate expression.

11 *glamour* – charm or fascination; the original meaning was a magic spell.

*Lawrence's diction – his choice of words – is particularly keen in this poem.
What are the associations suggested by 'glamour' in the last stanza, and
how does this word colour your view of the singer and the poet's memories?*

*How does the poet vary the length of the lines and place rhymes to suggest
the conflict in his mind?*

From *Look! We Have Come Through!*

These poems were written between 1912 and 1917. This is the point at
which Lawrence made the division between *Rhyming* and *Unrhyming Poems* in
his **Collected Poems**.

On the Balcony

This poem was originally titled *Illicit* in **Poetry** and was published in 1914.
The poem was also published in **Some Imagist Poets** in 1915. Lawrence and
Frieda were living south of Munich when it was written.

7 *limber* – able to move freely, agile.

9 *Adown* – below.

*Read the poem aloud and think carefully about the rhythm and the rhyme.
How are the lovers linked to the environment through the repetition of words
and through rhyme?*

*The landscape is both serene and turbulent. Do you think that is true of the
lovers' relationship also?*

In spite of myself, the insidious mastery of song
Betrays me back, till the heart of me weeps to belong
To the old Sunday evenings at home, with winter outside
And hymns in the cosy parlour, the tinkling piano our guide.

10 So now it is vain for the singer to burst into clamour
With the great black piano appassionato. The glamour
Of childish days is upon me, my manhood is cast
Down in the flood of remembrance, I weep like a child for the past.

From *Look! We Have Come Through!*

On the Balcony

In front of the sombre mountains, a faint, lost ribbon of rainbow;
And between us and it, the thunder;
And down below in the green wheat, the labourers
Stand like dark stumps, still in the green wheat.

5 You are near to me, and your naked feet in their sandals,
And through the scent of the balcony's naked timber
I distinguish the scent of your hair: so now the limber
Lightning falls from heaven.

Adown the pale-green glacier river floats
10 A dark boat through the gloom—and whither?
The thunder roars. But still we have each other!
The naked lightnings in the heavens dither
And disappear—what have we but each other?
The boat has gone.

Icking

A Youth Mowing

This poem was first published in **The Smart Set** under the title *The Mowers*.

1 *Isar* – a river in central Europe, flowing from Austria through Germany to the Danube.

2 *scythe* – a long-handled tool with a long, thin, curved blade, used for cutting hay or long grass.

8 *the trouble he's led to stall* – this vernacular (colloquial, local) phrase refers to the leading of animals to a stall or stable, but here means the trouble the youth is going to find (has brought home).

13 *scythe-stone* – the stone used to sharpen the blade of a scythe.

Describe the poet's feelings about the youth. What do they reveal about the poet?

What is the warning in the last stanza?

Examine Lawrence's use of vernacular language in this poem. Does it confuse or enhance the meaning?

A Doe At Evening

Like *A Youth Mowing*, this poem uses another, but different, deer image.

A Youth Mowing

There are four men mowing down by the Isar;
I can hear the swish of the scythe-strokes, four
Sharp breaths taken: yea, and I
Am sorry for what's in store.

5   The first man out of the four that's mowing
Is mine, I claim him once and for all;
Though it's sorry I am, on his young feet, knowing
None of the trouble he's led to stall.

As he sees me bringing the dinner, he lifts
10   His head as proud as a deer that looks
Shoulder-deep out of the corn; and wipes
His scythe-blade bright, unhooks

The scythe-stone and over the stubble to me.
Lad, thou has gotten a child in me,
15   Laddie, a man thou'lt ha'e to be,
Yea, though I'm sorry for thee.

A Doe at Evening

As I went through the marshes
a doe sprang out of the corn
and flashed up the hill-side
leaving her fawn.

5   On the sky-line
she moved round to watch,
she pricked a fine black blotch
on the sky.

What do the phrases 'level-balanced head' and 'head hard-balanced' refer to?

What do this poem and A Youth Mowing suggest about the poet's view of relationships between men and women?

Sunday Afternoon in Italy

In August–September 1912 Lawrence and Frieda travelled through Germany and Austria, and down to Italy. This poem is set in Gargnano, on the shores of Lake Garda. Here the poet channels his thoughts through his observation of the couple.

8   *cavil* – to quibble or make a petty objection.

I looked at her
10   and felt her watching;
I became a strange being.
Still, I had my right to be there with her.

Her nimble shadow trotting
along the sky-line, she
15   put back her fine, level-balanced head.
And I knew her.

Ah yes, being male, is not my head hard-balanced, antlered?
Are not my haunches light?
Has she not fled on the same wind with me?
20   Does not my fear cover her fear?

Irschenhausen

Sunday Afternoon in Italy

The man and the maid go side by side
With an interval of space between;
And his hands are awkward and want to hide,
She braves it out since she must be seen.

5   When some one passes he drops his head,
Shading his face in his black felt hat.
While the hard girl hardens; nothing is said,
There is nothing to wonder or cavil at.

Alone on the open road again,
10   With the mountain snows across the lake
Flushing the afternoon, they are uncomfortable,
The loneliness daunts them, their stiff throats ache.

18 *cordial* – polite or friendly.

35 *Wreathe* – to encircle or adorn with flowers and leaves. Now mostly associated with funeral wreaths, but also symbolizing fertility.

35 *enlap* – to enfold, protect.

35 *anoint* – to touch someone with sacred oil in a religious ceremony, as a sign of spiritual consecration or special dedication.

Why does the poet describe the gestures and expressions of the couple so clearly?

What are the differences between the men and the women in the poem? What is the poet's view of the women? Do you think he is afraid of them?

What is the effect of placing the last four stanzas in italics?

And he sighs with relief when she parts from him;
Her proud head held in its black silk scarf
15 Gone under the archway, home, he can join
The men that lounge in a group on the wharf.

His evening is a flame of wine
Among the eager, cordial men.
And she with her women hot and hard
20 Moves at her ease again.

> *She is marked, she is singled out*
>   *For the fire:*
> *The brand is upon him, look you!*
>   *Of desire.*

25   *They are chosen, ah, they are fated*
>   *For the fight!*
> *Champion her, all you women! Men, menfolk,*
>   *Hold him your light!*

> *Nourish her, train her, harden her,*
30   *Women all!*
> *Fold him, be good to him, cherish him,*
>   *Men, ere he fall.*

> *Women, another champion!*
>   *This, men, is yours!*
35 *Wreathe and enlap and anoint them*
>   *Behind separate doors.*

Gargnano

Giorno dei Morti

The title means 'Day of the Dead', which is 2 November, known in English as All Souls' Day. This descriptive poem was written in 1912 and first published in **The New Statesman** in 1913. It was later placed by Lawrence in the Look! We Have Come Through! cycle in **Collected Poems**. Here the poet sets out his poem in regular four-line stanzas and rhyming couplets.

16 *surplices* – loose white robes worn by clergy and choristers during services.

> How does the pattern of the poem echo the chanting of the service? (Look at the cadence – the rise and fall of the sound – and at repetition.)

Loggerheads

4 *See if they ring* – see if they are true (a reference to the difference in the sound made by real and counterfeit coins).

Giorno dei Morti

Along the avenue of cypresses,
All in their scarlet cloaks and surplices
Of linen, go the chanting choristers,
The priests in gold and black, the villagers....

5   And all along the path to the cemetery
The round dark heads of men crowd silently,
And black-scarved faces of womenfolk, wistfully
Watch at the banner of death, and the mystery.

And at the foot of a grave a father stands
10 With sunken head, and forgotten, folded hands;
And at the foot of a grave a mother kneels
With pale shut face, nor either hears nor feels

The coming of the chanting choristers
Between the avenue of cypresses,
15 The silence of the many villagers,
The candle-flames beside the surplices.

Loggerheads

Please yourself how you have it.
Take my words, and fling
Them down on the counter roundly;
See if they ring.

7   *sand in my doubtful sugar* – a reference to the practice of adulterating brown
    sugar with sand to bulk it up and so increase profits.

8   *verities* – truth(s).

What is the significance of the references to money in the poem?

What might the weeping willow symbolize?

Is there any sense in which the poem has a narrative and a setting? Do you
feel it might be a real or an imaginary scenario?

Coming Awake

This poem was written in 1913.

3   *primulas* – a plant like a primrose, with pink, purple, white or yellow
    flowers.

5   Sift my looks and expressions,
And see what proportion there is
Of sand in my doubtful sugar
Of verities.

Have a real stock-taking
10 Of my manly breast;
Find out if I'm sound or bankrupt,
Or a poor thing at best.

For I am quite indifferent
To your dubious state,
15 As to whether you've found a fortune
In me, or a flea-bitten fate.

Make a good investigation
Of all that is there,
And then, if it's worth it, be grateful—
20 If not, then despair.

If despair is our portion
Then let us despair.
Let us make for the weeping willow.
I don't care.

Coming Awake

When I woke, the lake-lights were quivering on the wall,
   The sunshine swam in a shoal across and across,
And a hairy, big bee hung over the primulas
   In the window, his body black fur, and the sound of him cross.

What distracts the poet from the bee?

Do you think that the metaphor of the sun as a shoal is effective? In what way(s)?

Discuss whether the rhymes add anything to the meaning of the poem.

People

This poem strikes a note of cynicism often found in some of Lawrence's other poems set in urban environments such as *In The Cities* (see page 135).

  2 *bough* – a large branch, usually starting from the tree trunk.

  7 *sough* – a sigh or murmur.

  11 *Ghost-flux* – ghostly and flowing movement.
  11 *hie* – archaic verb meaning 'hurry' or 'hasten'.

What are the 'apples of night'?

From *Birds, Beasts and Flowers*

The poems in this collection were written mainly between September 1920 and Spring 1923. Most date from Lawrence's stay in Sicily.

From *Fruits*

Peace

Taormina is a town at the foot of Mount Etna, an active volcano in east Sicily.

5 There was something I ought to remember: and yet
  I did not remember. Why should I? The running lights
  And the airy primulas, oblivious
  Of the impending bee—they were fair enough sights.

People

  The great gold apples of night
  Hang from the street's long bough
     Dripping their light
  On the faces that drift below,
5 On the faces that drift and blow
  Down the night-time, out of sight
     In the wind's sad sough.

  The ripeness of these apples of night
  Distilling over me
10   Makes sickening the white
  Ghost-flux of faces that hie
  Them endlessly, endlessly by
  Without meaning or reason why
     They ever should be.

From *Birds, Beasts and Flowers*

Peace

  Peace is written on the doorstep
  In lava.

  Peace, black peace congealed.
  My heart will know no peace
5 Till the hill bursts.

11 *Naxos* – the ancient centre for the worship of Dionysos, the Greek god of wine, fertility and vegetation (see *Middle of the World*, page 129).

How does the cadence in the poem rise and fall? What effect does this have on the mood and tone of the poem?

What sort of peace is offered by the lava?

From *Flowers*

From: *Hibiscus and Salvia Flowers*

This extract gives the flavour of an extended poem that describes Lawrence's thinking after coming face to face with Italian socialism.

Brilliant, intolerable lava,
Brilliant as a powerful burning-glass,
Walking like a royal snake down the mountain towards the sea.

Forests, cities, bridges
10 Gone again in the bright trail of lava.
Naxos thousands of feet below the olive-roots,
And now the olive leaves thousands of feet below the lava fire.

Peace congealed in black lava on the doorstep.
Within, white-hot lava, never at peace
15 Till it burst forth blinding, withering the earth;
To set again into rock,
Grey-black rock.

Call it Peace?

Taormina

From *Hibiscus and Salvia Flowers*

Hark! Hark!
The dogs do bark!
It's the socialists come to town,
None in rags and none in tags,
5 *Swaggering up and down.*

Sunday morning,
And from the Sicilian townlets skirting Etna
The socialists have gathered upon us, to look at us.

How shall we know them when we see them?
10 How shall we know them now they've come?

16   the *Corso* – the main street in an Italian town.

19   *forestière* – French word for forester or woodcutter; perhaps a specific
      example of the 'lordly tuppenny foreigners' referred to in the next line.

20   *tuppenny* – worthless, jumped-up (literally, worth two pence, or less
      than 1p in modern currency).

29-32 *Bolshevists. Leninists. Communists. Socialists.* – at this time, these different
      groups stood for slightly different interpretations of the revolutionary
      ideas of Karl Marx.

34   *salvia and hibiscus flowers* – salvia is a garden plant belonging to the sage
      family, with bright red or blue flowers, and hibiscus is a tropical shrub
      cultivated for its bright red flowers.

The refrain in italics is reminiscent of a nursery rhyme. What effect does it
have on the overall tone of the poem?

Not by their rags and not by their tags,
Nor by any distinctive gown;
The same unremarkable Sunday suit
And hats cocked up and down.

15 Yet there they are, youths, loutishly
Strolling in gangs and staring along the Corso
With the gang-stare
And a half-threatening envy
At every *forestière*,
20 Every lordly tuppenny foreigner from the hotels, fattening on the
    exchange.

Hark! Hark!
The dogs do bark!
It's the socialists in the town.

25 Sans rags, sans tags,
Sans beards, sans bags,
Sans any distinction at all except loutish commonness.

How do we know then, that they are they?
Bolshevists.
30 Leninists.
Communists.
Socialists.
-Ists! -Ists!

· Alas, salvia and hibiscus flowers.
35 Salvia and hibiscus flowers.

Listen again.
Salvia and hibiscus flowers.
Is it not so?
Salvia and hibiscus flowers.

48   *perambulating* – walking or strolling.

52   *Azalea and camellia* – azalea is a shrub closely related to the
      rhododendron, with bright red, pink or purple flowers, and camellia is
      an ornamental shrub with rose-like flowers.

53   *mallow-flower* – a plant of the same family as hibiscus.

61   *filigreed* – as a noun, filigree is delicate ornamental work made of gold or
      silver wire. Here Lawrence uses it as an adjective.

Note down phrases or words which show the development of the metaphor
comparing the Socialists to the salvia and hibiscus flowers. What point is
the poet making with this comparison?

Why does the poet allude to Eve and her role in the fall of mankind?

40 *Hark! Hark!*
    The dogs do bark!
    Salvia and hibiscus flowers.

    Who smeared their doors with blood?
    Who on their breasts
45 Put salvias and hibiscus

    Rosy, rosy scarlet.
    And flame-rage, golden-throated
    Bloom along the Corso on the living, perambulating bush.

    Who said they might assume these blossoms?
50 What god did they consult?

    Rose-red, princess hibiscus, rolling her pointed Chinese petals!
    Azalea and camellia, single peony
    And pomegranate bloom and scarlet mallow-flower
    And all the eastern, exquisite royal plants
55 That noble blood has brought us down the ages!
    Gently nurtured, frail and splendid
    Hibiscus flower—
    Alas, the Sunday coats of Sicilian bolshevists!

    Pure blood, and noble blood, in the fine and rose-red veins;
60 Small, interspersed with jewels of white gold
    Frail-filigreed among the rest;
    Rose of the oldest races of princesses, Polynesian
    Hibiscus.

    Eve, in her happy moments,
65   Put hibiscus in her hair,
    Before she humbled herself, and knocked her knees with repentance.

    Sicilian bolshevists,
    With hibiscus flowers in the buttonholes of your Sunday suits,
    Come now, speaking of rights, what right have you to this flower?

73 *noblesse oblige* – this often ironic phrase refers to the supposed
obligation of the nobility to be honourable and generous.

What is Lawrence's attitude towards the Socialists? Does it change at all
throughout the poem? Does he support their ideals, or is there a sense of
irony at the end of the poem – or both?

From *Creatures*

Mosquito

The poem was written in Sicily in May 1920 and first published in the New
York **Bookman** in July 1921. Lawrence explores his physical and mental
attitude towards this blood-sucking insect with real effect. He does not
dismiss the insect but wryly contemplates its appearance and role.

Why does Lawrence use the greeting 'Monsieur' in line 2 and how does it set
the tone for the start of the poem?

5 *exaltation* – a raising or lifting up of rank or honour; a rapture or
excitement.

9 *Winged Victory* – a famous statue of Nike, the Greek goddess of victory,
depicted as a woman or spirit with wings.

Why do you think that 'the Winged Victory' is such an apt description of the
mosquito in this poem?

Can you say why the connection of the mosquito with Venice might be
particularly appropriate? Or why the poet describes the city as 'sluggish'?

70 The exquisite and ageless aristocracy
Of a peerless soul,
Blessed are the pure in heart and the fathomless in bright pride;
The loveliness that knows *noblesse oblige*;
The native royalty of red hibiscus flowers;
75 The exquisite assertion of new delicate life
Risen from the roots:
Is this how you'll have it, red-decked socialists,
Hibiscus-breasted?
If it be so, I fly to join you,
80 And if it be not so, brutes to pull down hibiscus flowers!

Taormina

Mosquito

When did you start your tricks,
Monsieur?

What do you stand on such high legs for?
Why this length of shredded shank,
5 You exaltation?

Is it so that you shall lift your centre of gravity upwards
And weigh no more than air as you alight upon me,
Stand upon me weightless, you phantom?

I heard a woman call you the Winged Victory
10 In sluggish Venice.
You turn your head towards your tail, and smile.

How can you put so much devilry
Into that translucent phantom shred
Of a frail corpus?

18   *aura* – an invisible emanation or atmosphere.

26   *Ghoul* – a malevolent ghost or a person who robs graves. In Muslim
      legend, a spirit which preys on graves and eats corpses.

38   *trump* – an archaic or literary word for the sound of a
      trumpet.

15   Queer, with your thin wings and your streaming legs,
     How you sail like a heron, or a dull clot of air,
     A nothingness.

     Yet what an aura surrounds you;
     Your evil little aura, prowling, and casting numbness on my mind.
20   That is your trick, your bit of filthy magic:
     Invisibility, and the anæsthetic power
     To deaden my attention in your direction.

     But I know your game now, streaky sorcerer.
     Queer, how you stalk and prowl the air
25   In circles and evasions, enveloping me,
     Ghoul on wings
     Winged Victory.

     Settle, and stand on long thin shanks
     Eyeing me sideways, and cunningly conscious that I am aware,
30   You speck.

     I hate the way you lurch off sideways into the air
     Having read my thoughts against you.

     Come then, let us play at unawares,
     And see who wins in this sly game of bluff.
35   Man or mosquito.

     You don't know that I exist, and I don't know that you exist.
     Now then!

     It is your trump,
     It is your hateful little trump,
40   You pointed fiend,
     Which shakes my sudden blood to hatred of you:
     It is your small, high, hateful bugle in my ear.

54-55   *enspasmed* and *ecstasied* – Lawrence has coined two new words here,
         the one from 'spasm' and the other from 'ecstasy', both emphasizing
         the sudden state of delight and bliss the insect feels.

67   *paean* – a song or shout of praise or triumph (from the Greek).

Why do you do it?
Surely it is bad policy,
45 They say you can't help it.

If that is so, then I believe a little in Providence protecting the
    innocent.
But it sounds so amazingly like a slogan,
A yell of triumph as you snatch my scalp.

50 Blood, red blood
Super-magical
Forbidden liquor.

I behold you stand
For a second enspasmed in oblivion,
55 Obscenely ecstasied
Sucking live blood,
My blood.

Such silence, such suspended transport,
Such gorging,
60 Such obscenity of trespass.

You stagger
As well as you may.
Only your accursed hairy frailty,
Your own imponderable weightlessness
65 Saves you, wafts you away on the very draught my anger makes
    in its snatching.

Away with a pæan of derision,
You winged blood-drop.
Can I not overtake you?

70 Are you one too many for me,
Winged Victory?
Am I not mosquito enought to out-mosquito you?

Bat

This poem was published in **English Review** in November 1921.

3   *Carrara* – the mountainous area in central Italy.

7   *Ponte Vecchio* – 'The Old Bridge' is a famous mid fourteenth-century bridge with shops that spans the river Arno in Florence.

13   *parabola* – a curving trajectory.

Queer what a big stain my sucked blood makes
Beside the infinitesimal faint smear of you!
75 Queer, what a dim dark smudge you have disappeared into!

Siracusa

Bat

At evening, sitting on this terrace,
When the sun from the west, beyond Pisa, beyond the mountains of
    Carrara
Depart, and the world is taken by surprise...

5 When the tired flower of Florence is in gloom beneath the glowing
Brown hills surrounding...
When under the arches of the Ponte Vecchio
A green light enters against stream, flush from the west,
Against the current of obscure Arno...

10 Look up, and you see things flying
Between the day and the night;
Swallows with spools of dark thread sewing the shadows together.

A circle swoop, and a quick parabola under the bridge arches
Where light pushes through;
15 A sudden turning upon itself of a thing in the air.
A dip to the water.

And you think:
"The swallows are flying so late!"

Swallows?

40 *Pipistrello* – the Italian word for a bat.

How does Lawrence mix disgust, admiration and humour in this poem?

How does Lawrence use colour and movement to enhance the detail and feel of the poem?

20 Dark air-life looping
Yet missing the pure loop...
A twitch, a twitter, an elastic shudder in flight
And serrated wings against the sky,
Like a glove, a black glove thrown up at the light,
25 And falling back.

Never swallows!
Bats!
The swallows are gone.

At a wavering instant the swallows give way to bats
30 By the Ponte Vecchio...
Changing guard.

Bats, and an uneasy creeping in one's scalp
As the bats swoop overhead!
Flying madly.

40 Pipistrello!
Black piper on an infinitesimal pipe.
Little lumps that fly in air and have voices indefinite, wildly
    vindictive;

Wings like bits of umbrella.

50 Bats!

Creatures that hang themselves up like an old rag, to sleep;
And disgustingly upside down.
Hanging upside down like rows of disgusting old rags
And grinning in their sleep.
55 Bats!

In China the bat is symbol of happiness.

Not for me!

From *Reptiles*

Snake

Snake

Written in July 1920 and first published in ***Dial*** in July 1921, this is one of Lawrence's best-known poems. It was collected in ***Georgian Poetry***. The poem was written during the poet's two-year stay in Sicily and is based on his encounter with a snake in Taormina. Snakes were revered in ancient, pagan myth as gods of the underworld and so were associated with death. Lawrence sees the dignity and simple beauty of the creature.

4   *carob-tree* – an evergreen Mediterranean tree with edible seed pods.

8   *fissure* – the snake emerges from a narrow crack in the wall.

25   *Etna* – Mount Etna is an active volcano in eastern Sicily.

Snake

A snake came to my water-trough
On a hot, hot day, and I in pyjamas for the heat,
To drink there.

In the deep, strange-scented shade of the great dark carob-tree
5   I came down the steps with my pitcher
And must wait, must stand and wait, for there he was at the trough
    before me.

He reached down from a fissure in the earth-wall in the gloom
And trailed his yellow-brown slackness soft-bellied down, over the
    edge of the stone trough
10 And rested his throat upon the stone bottom,
And where the water had dripped from the tap, in a small clearness,
He sipped with his straight mouth,
Softly drank through his straight gums, into his slack long body,
15 Silently.

Someone was before me at my water-trough,
And I, like a second comer, waiting.

He lifted his head from his drinking, as cattle do,
And looked at me vaguely, as drinking cattle do,
20 And flickered his two-forked tongue from his lips, and mused a
    moment,
And stooped and drank a little more,
Being earth-brown, earth-golden from the burning bowels of the
    earth
25 On the day of Sicilian July, with Etna smoking.

53 *adream* – dreaming, in a trance.

The voice of my education said to me
He must be killed,
For in Sicily the black, black snakes are innocent, the gold are
    venomous.

30 And voices in me said, If you were a man
You would take a stick and break him now, and finish him off.

But must I confess how I liked him,
How glad I was he had come like a guest in quiet, to drink at my
    water-trough
35 And depart peaceful, pacified, and thankless,
Into the burning bowels of this earth?

Was it cowardice, that I dared not kill him?
Was it perversity, that I longed to talk to him?
Was it humility, to feel so honoured?
40 I felt so honoured.

And yet those voices:
If you were not afraid, you would kill him!

And truly I was afraid, I was most afraid,
But even so, honoured still more
45 That he should seek my hospitality
From out the dark door of the secret earth.

He drank enough
And lifted his head, dreamily, as one who has drunken,
And flickered his tongue like a forked night on the air, so black;
50 Seeming to lick his lips,
And looked around like a god, unseeing, into the air,
And slowly turned his head,
And slowly, very slowly, as if thrice adream,
Proceeded to draw his slow length curving round
60 And climb again the broken bank of my wall-face.

81 *albatross* – in *The Rime of the Ancient Mariner* by Coleridge, an albatross is
shot by the mariner and by so doing he brings a curse on himself and
his ship.

86-7 *one of the lords of life* – a visionary perception of the snake's God-given
beauty and integrity.

88 *expiate* – to make amends for.

*How is the snake built up to appear as one of the 'lords of life'? Why does
Lawrence stop and measure his worth and power against that of the snake?*

*How does the persona of the educated voice contrast with the affinity the
poet feels with the snake?*

Compare the poet's attitude to the two creatures in Snake and Mosquito.

And as he put his head into that dreadful hole,
And as he slowly drew up, snake-easing his shoulders, and entered
    farther,
A sort of horror, a sort of protest against his withdrawing into
that horrid black hole,
65 Deliberately going into the blackness, and slowly drawing himself
    after,
Overcame me now his back was turned.

I looked round, I put down my pitcher,
70 I picked up a clumsy log
And threw it at the water-trough with a clatter.
I think it did not hit him,
But suddenly that part of him that was left behind convulsed in
    undignified haste,
75 Writhed like lightning, and was gone
Into the black hole, the earth-lipped fissure in the wall-front,
At which, in the intense still noon, I stared with fascination.

And immediately I regretted it.
I thought how paltry, how vulgar, what a mean act!
80 I despised myself and the voices of my accursed human education

And I thought of the albatross,
And I wished he would come back, my snake.

For he seemed to me again like a king,
Like a king in exile, uncrowned in the underworld,
85 Now due to be crowned again.

And so, I missed my chance with one of the lords
Of life.
And I have something to expiate;
A pettiness.

Taormina

Tortoise Family Connections

This poem was written in the early autumn of 1920 and was part of a
sequence called *Tortoises* published in 1921 in New York and later included
in **Birds, Beasts and Flowers**. Here Lawrence starts off by musing with
wonder and joy on the process of creation.

3   *Pediment* – in architecture, a triangular gable on top of a portico,
    doorway or window.

14 *Woman...thee* – a Biblical quotation, Christ's words to his mother in
    John ɪɪ 4.

19 *incognisant* – unaware.

25 *irascible* – irritable.

Tortoise Family Connections

On he goes, the little one,
Bud of the universe,
Pediment of life.

Setting off somewhere, apparently.
5 Whither away, brisk egg?

His mother deposited him on the soil as if he were no more than
  droppings,
And now he scuffles tinily past her as if she were an old rusty tin.

A mere obstacle,
10 He veers round the slow great mound of her—
Tortoises always forsee obstacles.

It is no use my saying to him in an emotional voice:
"This is your Mother, she laid you when you were an egg."

He does not even trouble to answer: "Woman, what have I to do
  with thee?"
15 He wearily looks the other way,
And she even more wearily looks another way still,
Each with the utmost apathy,
Incognisant,
20 Unaware,
Nothing.

As for papa,
He snaps when I offer him his offspring,
Just as he snaps when I poke a bit of stick at him,
25 Because he is irascible this morning, an irascible tortoise
Being touched with love, and devoid of fatherliness.

47   *Basta* – enough (in Italian).

How does Lawrence contrast the behaviour of the tortoises with that of
human parents?

How does the poet use satire to contrast the tortoise with proud human
beings?

Father and mother,
And three little brothers,
And all rambling aimless, like little perambulating pebbles scattered
   in the garden,
30 Not knowing each other from bits of earth or old tins.

Except that papa and mama are old acquaintances, of course,
Though family feeling there is none, not even the beginnings.
Fatherless, motherless, brotherless, sisterless
Little tortoise.

35 Row on then, small pebble,
Over the clods of the autumn, wind-chilled sunshine,
Young gaiety.

Does he look for a companion?

No, no, don't think it.
40 He doesn't know he is alone;
Isolation is his birthright,
This atom.

To row forward, and reach himself tall on spiny toes,
To travel, to burrow into a little loose earth, afraid of the night,
45 To crop a little substance,
To move, and to be quite sure that he is moving:
Basta!
To be a tortoise!
Think of it, in a garden of inert clods
50 A brisk, brindled little tortoise, all to himself—
Adam!

In a garden of pebbles and insects
To roam, and feel the slow heart beat
Tortoise-wise, the first bell sounding
55 From the warm blood, in the dark-creation morning.

58   *stoic* – a person who reveals endurance and courage shows the qualities
     encouraged by the Stoics, a Greek philosophical sect who believed that
     happiness can only be achieved if one submits to destiny and natural
     law.

How does the tortoise find its own individuality?

What is the implied contrast between the stoic tortoise and the surrounding
chaos in the last stanza?

From *Birds*

Humming-Bird

First published in the American magazine **New Republic** in 1921, this poem
was written in Sicily: Lawrence later gave it the place name 'Española', to
record the place where he first saw humming-birds, in 1923.

2   *primeval* – from prehistoric times.

6   *Matter* – any physical substance that exists in time and space and is
    affected by gravity.

How do lines 7 and 8 suggest the speed and darting agility of the
humming-bird?

What is Lawrence alluding to in the phrase 'the slow vegetable veins' in line
11?

What threat does the image of the large primitive and primeval bird
embody? How has Time changed the balance between humans and the
power of Nature?

Moving, and being himself,
Slow, and unquestioned,
And inordinately there, O stoic!
Wandering in the slow triumph of his own existence,
60   Ringing the soundless bell of his presence in chaos,
And biting the frail grass arrogantly,
Decidedly arrogantly.

Humming-Bird

I can imagine, in some other world
Primeval-dumb, far back
In that most awful stillness, that only gasped and hummed,
Humming-birds raced down the avenues.

5   Before anything had a soul,
While life was a heave of Matter, half inanimate,
This little bit chipped off in brilliance
And went whizzing through the slow, vast, succulent stems.

I believe there were no flowers then,
10   In the world where the humming-bird flashed ahead of creation.
I believe he pierced the slow vegetable veins with his long beak.

Probably he was big
As mosses, and little lizards, they say, were once big.
Probably he was jabbing, terrifying monster.

15   We look at him through the wrong end of the long telescope
        of Time,
Luckily for us.

Española

Eagle in New Mexico

This rather disturbing poem reveals some of Lawrence's interest in the ritual death and resurrection beliefs of Mexico and New Mexico. The Aztecs, a highly cultured civilization, were also an extremely warlike and strictly hierarchical society. The priests led a monthly festival where human victims, usually prisoners of war, were sacrificed by tearing out their living hearts, which were believed to be essential food for the gods. The life-giving blood renewed the gods and ensured that the 'new fire' of the sun-god was kept alight during the cycle of the solar year. Wars had to be waged to provide the often thousands of lives needed.

5 *eagle* – the eagle is the national bird of the USA.

6 *sage-ash* – a local bush or small tree.

9 *pallid* – pale.

What do you think Lawrence means by 'the inner eye' (line 28)?

Eagle in New Mexico

Towards the sun, towards the south-west
A scorched breast.
A scorched breast, breasting the sun like an answer,
Like a retort.

5 An eagle at the top of a low cedar-bush
On the sage-ash desert
Reflecting the scorch of the sun from his breast;
Eagle, with the sickle dripping darkly above.

Erect, scorched-pallid out of the hair of the cedar,
10 Erect, with the god-thrust entering him from below,
Eagle gloved in feathers
In scorched white feathers
In burnt dark feathers
In feathers still fire-rusted;
15 Sickle-overswept, sickle dripping over and above.

Sun-breaster,
Staring two ways at once, to right and left;
Masked-one
Dark-visaged
20 Sickle-masked
With iron between your two eyes;
You feather-gloved
To the feet;
Foot-fierce;
25 Erect one;
The god-thrust entering you steadily from below.

You never look at the sun with your two eyes.
Only the inner eye of your scorched broad breast
Looks straight at the sun.

34   *Damocles* – in Greek myth, Damocles' own sword was suspended
      above him on a hair by king Dionysius, the tyrant of Syracuse, to show
      that being a monarch was a precarious position to be in.

*Explain your feelings about the ancient blood sacrifices of the Aztec
Civilization or the eagle's view of life.*

30 You are dark
    Except scorch-pale-breasted;
    And dark cleaves down and weapon-hard downward curving
    At your scorched breast,
    Like a sword of Damocles,
35 Beaked eagle.

    You've dipped it in blood so many times
    That dark face-weapon, to temper it well,
    Blood-thirsty bird.

    Why do you front the sun so obstinately,
40 American eagle?
    As if you owed him an old, old grudge, great sun: or an old, old
      allegiance.

    When you pick the red smoky heart from a rabbit or a light-
      blooded bird
45 Do you lift it to the sun, as the Aztec priests used to lift red hearts
      of men?

    Does the sun need steam of blood do you think
    In America, still,
    Old eagle?

50 Does the sun in New Mexico sail like a fiery bird of prey in the sky
    Hovering?

    Does he shriek for blood?
    Does he fan great wings above the prairie, like a hovering, blood-
      thirsty bird?

55 And are you his priest, big eagle
    Whom the Indians aspire to?
    Is there a bond of bloodshed between you?

68   *chastened* – to be punished by suffering.

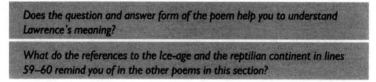

Does the question and answer form of the poem help you to understand Lawrence's meaning?

What do the references to the Ice-age and the reptilian continent in lines 59–60 remind you of in the other poems in this section?

The Blue Jay

This poem was written in New Mexico in the winter of 1922–3, when Lawrence and Frieda were living on a ranch in the foothills of the Rocky Mountains.

Is your continent cold from the ice-age still, that the sun is so angry?
Is the blood of your continent somewhat reptilian still,
60 That the sun should be greedy for it?

I don't yield to you, big, jowl-faced eagle.
Nor you nor your blood-thirsty sun
That sucks up blood
Leaving a nervous people.

65 Fly off, big bird with a big black back.
Fly slowly away, with a rust of fire in your tail,
Dark as you are on your dark side, eagle of heaven.

Even the sun in heaven can be curbed and chastened at last
By the life in the hearts of men.
70 And you, great bird, sun-starer, heavy black beak
Can be put out of office as sacrifice bringer.

                                                    Taos

The Blue Jay

The blue jay with a crest on his head
Comes round the cabin in the snow.
He runs in the snow like a bit of blue metal,
Turning his back on everything.

5 From the pine-tree that towers and hisses like a pillar of shaggy
        cloud
Immense above the cabin
Comes a strident laugh as we approach, this little black dog and I.
So halts the little black bitch on four spread paws in the snow

13   *What voice...smoke* – a Biblical reference from Exodus III 2, which
     relates how God spoke to Moses from the burning bush.

If God is speaking to Lawrence through the jay, why is there a sense that the bird (and possibly God) is ridiculing the poet?

From *Animals*

Kangaroo

Lawrence visited Australia in May–August 1922. The strange marsupial animals and unusual physical features of the sub-continent fascinated him.

10   And looks up inquiringly into the pillar of cloud,
      With a tinge of misgiving.
      Ca-a-a! comes the scrape of ridicule out of the tree.

      What voice of the Lord is that, from the tree of smoke?

      Oh, Bibbles, little black bitch in the snow,
15   With a pinch of snow in the groove of your silly snub nose,
      What do you look at *me* for?
      What do you look at me for, with such misgiving?

      It's the blue jay laughing at us.
      It's the blue jay jeering at us, Bibs.

20   Every day since the snow is here
      The blue jay paces round the cabin, very busy, picking up bits,
      Turning his back on us all,
      And bobbing his thick dark crest about the snow, as if darkly
         saying:
25   *I ignore those folk who look out.*

      You acid-blue metallic bird,
      You thick bird with a strong crest,
      Who are you?
      Whose boss are you, with all your bully way?
30   You copper-sulphate blue bird!

                                               Lobo

Kangaroo

      In the northern hemisphere
      Life seems to leap at the air, or skim under the wind
      Like stags on rocky ground, or pawing horses, or springy scut-tailed
         rabbits.

14 *antipodal* – from the antipodes, which literally means a country or region directly opposite to one's own.

21 *plumb-weighted* – a plumb is a ball of lead, or other metal, fixed to a line to test vertical depth and alignment.

30 *Victorian shoulders* – Victorian women are often portrayed with sloping shoulders, which was the fashionable and admired body shape of the time.

5   Or else rush horizontal to charge at the sky's horizon,
Like bulls or bisons or wild pigs.

Or slip like water slippery towards its ends,
As foxes, stoats, and wolves, and prairie dogs.

Only mice, and moles, and rats, and badgers, and beavers, and
10   perhaps bears
Seem belly-plumbed to the earth's mid-navel.
Or frogs that when they leap come flop, and flop to the centre
   of the earth.

But the yellow antipodal Kangaroo, when she sits up,
15 Who can unseat her, like a liquid drop that is heavy, and just
   touches earth.

The downward drip
The down-urge.
So much denser than cold-blooded frogs.

20 Delicate mother Kangaroo
Sitting up there rabbit-wise, but huge, plumb-weighted,
And lifting her beautiful slender face, oh! so much more gently and
   finely lined than a rabbit's, or than a hare's,
Lifting her face to nibble at a round white peppermint drop which
25 she loves, sensitive mother Kangaroo.

Her sensitive, long, pure-bred face,
Her full antipodal eyes, so dark,
So big and quiet and remote, having watched so many empty dawns
   in silent Australia.

30 Her little loose hands, and drooping Victorian shoulders.
And then her great weight below the waist, her vast pale belly
With a thin young yellow little paw hanging out, and straggle of a
   long thin ear, like ribbon,
Like a funny trimming to the middle of her belly, thin little dangle
35 of an immature paw, and one thin ear.

56 *land of the South* – before Australia was discovered, the unknown regions of the southern hemisphere were shown on maps as Terra Australis, or 'Land of the South'.

58 *lowed* – the hollow, bellowing sound of cattle.

*What does the kangaroo's tail described as a 'python-stretch' in line 37 remind you of in other poems from **Birds, Beasts and Flowers**?*

What is your reaction to the passing reference to the Aborigines in lines 51–3?

Her belly, her big haunches
And, in addition, the great muscular python-stretch of her tail.

There, she shan't have any more peppermint drops.
So she wistfully, sensitively sniffs the air, and then turns, goes off in
40   slow sad leaps

On the long flat skis of her legs,
Steered and propelled by that steel-strong snake of a tail.

Stops again, half turns, inquisitive to look back.
While something stirs quickly in her belly, and a lean little face
45   comes out, as from a window,
Peaked and a bit dismayed,
Only to disappear again quickly away from the sight of the world, to
    snuggle down in the warmth,
Leaving the trail of a different paw hanging out.

50 Still she watches with eternal, cocked wistfulness!
How full her eyes are, like the full, fathomless, shining eyes of an
    Australian black-boy
Who has been lost so many centuries on the margins of existence!

She watches with insatiable wistfulness.
55 Untold centuries of watching for something to come,
For a new signal from life, in that silent lost land of the South.

Where nothing bites but insects and snakes and the sun, small life.
Where no bull roared, no cow ever lowed, no stag cried, no leopard
    screeched, no lion coughed, no dog barked,
60 But all was silent save for parrots occasionally, in the haunted blue
    bush.

How does the poet's approach to the kangaroo compare with his attitude towards the subject of Snake?

Beyond the Rockies

Lawrence wrote few poems in the mid-1920s. According to Lawrence's diary this poem was written in Spotorno, Italy, in February 1926 and then published in **Laughing Horse** in April. It was an uncollected piece and found after his death. The Rocky Mountains or Rockies stretch from Alaska through North America to Mexico.

7   *winding-sheet* – a cloth which wraps a corpse. American Indians were buried in the blanket they wore in life.

In what ways does the chain of mountains divide the Mexican Indians from the people in the 'west'?

Wistfully watching, with wonderful liquid eyes.
And all her weight, all her blood, dripping sack-wise down
   towards the earth's centre,
65   And the live little-one taking in its paw at the door of her belly.

Leap then, and come down on the line that draws to the earth's
   deep, heavy centre.

Sydney

Beyond the Rockies

There are people there, beyond the Rockies
As there are people here, on this side.

But the people there, beyond the Rockies
Seem always to be asking, asking something.

5   The new moon sets at sundown,
And there, beyond the sunset, quivers.

An Indian, walking wrapt in his winding sheet
Answers the question as he puts it, in his stride.

Mexicans, like people who have died
10   Ask, in the space of their eyes:
What have we lost?

What have we lost, in the west?
We who have gone west?
There is no answer.

15   In the land of the lost
Nothing but to make lost music.

What images does line 17 evoke for you?

How do the repetitions of 'lost' reinforce the point of the poem?

From *Pansies* and *More Pansies*

The poems which follow are taken from **Pansies**, which Lawrence desribed collectively as 'a bunch of fragments' and thoughts. Lawrence got the idea for these pieces from *Pensées*, a collection of fragments of Christian apologia – a formal justification – by the seventeenth-century French philosopher Pascal, but 'pansies' is also a punning anglicization of 'pensées', the French word for thoughts.

The first poems were written between November and December 1928, in Bandol, France. The typescript of the collection was seized by the police but was later published with deletions in July 1929. The missing 14 poems were published privately in August 1929. Others followed in **More Pansies**, published after the poet's death in the collection **Last Poems**.

Elephants in the Circus

These poems are from a sequence about elephants.

   2   *aeons* – an immensely long time.

Two Performing Elephants

   2   *pallid* – pale, lacking in colour or energy.

   2   *hoary* – having grey or white hair, especially in old age.

   5   *agog* – eager or excited.

On the rim of the desert
Round the lost man's camp-fire
Watch the new moon
20   Curved, cut the last threads.

It is finished: the rest is afterwards
With grey on the floor of the desert,
And more space than in life.

From *Pansies* and *More Pansies*

Elephants in the Circus

Elephants in the circus
have æons of weariness round their eyes.
Yet they sit up
and show vast bellies to the children.

Two Performing Elephants

He stands with his forefeet on the drum
and the other, the old one, the pallid hoary female
must creep her great bulk beneath the bridge of him.

On her knees, in utmost caution
5   all agog, and curling up her trunk
she edges through without upsetting him.
Triumph! the ancient, pig-tailed monster!

When her trick is to climb over him
with what shadow-like slow carefulness
10   she skims him, sensitive
as shadows from the ages gone and perished
in touching him, and planting her round feet.

Why do you think the poet chose to explore his ideas on the same subject more than once?

Destiny

5 *pterodactyl* – an extinct flying reptile.

7 *extant* – still existing.

Is this poem in any sense rhetorical – is the initial question asked in order to create an effect rather than to provoke an answer?

A Living

The following four poems use free verse in order to explore the so-called 'achievements' of 'mankind'. In *A Living* Lawrence compares the carefree existence of the bird with human life. Lawrence wrote in a letter to Charles Wilson, in 1928, 'Let money and work be as casual in human life as they are in a bird's', which is the idea that forms the theme of this poem.

5 *heedless* – unworried, without concern or caution.

While the wispy, modern children, half-afraid
watch silent. The looming of the hoary, far-gone ages
15   is too much for them.

Destiny

O destiny, destiny,
do you exist, and can a man touch your hand?
O destiny
if I could see your hand, and it were thumbs down,
5   I would be willing to give way, like the pterodactyl,
and accept obliteration.
I would not even ask to leave a fossil claw extant,
nor a thumb-mark like a clue,
I would be willing to vanish completely, completely.

10   But if it is thumbs up, and mankind must go on being mankind,
then I am willing to fight, I will roll my sleeves up
and start in.

Only, O destiny
I wish you'd show your hand.

A Living

A man should never earn his living,
if he earns his life he'll be lovely.

A bird
picks up its seeds or little snails
5   between heedless earth and heaven
in heedlessness.

8   *chirruping* – chirping, short high-pitched sounds.

> *How successfully do lines 7-10 suggest a sense of fun? Is Lawrence in any way patronizing the bird?*

> *What is the message in this poem?*

Things Men Have Made –

This poem was originally published in **Dial** in July 1929.

> *How do the things made in the past and mentioned in this poem compare or contrast with Lawrence's attitude to the mechanical modern world?*

> *In what way is the poem nostalgic?*

Let Us Be Men –

This poem functions as a 'call to arms' and epitomizes Lawrence's attitude to the modern world.

> *How effective is Lawrence's use of the monkey image in the poem? How does his representation of the monkey contrast with his usual attitude towards animals?*

> *What is Lawrence objecting to in human behaviour here?*

But, the plucky little sport, it gives to life
song, and chirruping, gay feathers, fluff-shadowed warmth
and all the unspeakable charm of birds hopping and fluttering and
10   being birds.
—And we, we get it all from them for nothing.

Things Men Have Made—

Things men have made with wakened hands, and put soft life into
are awake through years with transferred touch, and go on glowing
for long years.
And for this reason, some old things are lovely
warm still with the life of forgotten men who made them.

Let Us Be Men—

For God's sake, let us be men
not monkeys minding machines
or sitting with our tails curled
while the machine amuses us, the radio or film or gramophone.

Monkeys with a bland grin on our faces.—

What is He?

What is he?
—A man, of course.
Yes, but what does he do?
—He lives and is a man.

What is He?

7   *leisured classes* – this phrase encompasses all those in society who, with a private income or wealth based on assets, have no need to work. It is almost always used in a derogatory sense.

19   *flautist* – flute player.

> What makes What is He? *a poem rather than prose?*

> Are there any other poems in the selection that express Lawrence's feelings about social class?

> How do the four poems in this group relate to each other? Are they reflections of separate ideas, or simply different strands of the same idea?

> Comment on the acerbity – the sharp and bitter aspects – of the poet's views in these poems.

Spray

This poem and *Sea-Weed* examine the beauty and power of the sea.

3   *sibilant* – hissing.

> What sort of anger is Lawrence hinting at in this poem?

> What aspects of human experience might this poem reflect?

5   Oh quite! but he must work. He must have a job of some sort.
    —Why?
    Because obviously he's not one of the leisured classes.
    —I don't know. He has lots of leisure. And he makes quite beautiful
      chairs.—
10 There you are then! He's a cabinet maker.
    —No no!
    Anyhow a carpenter and joiner.
    —Not at all.
    But you said so.
15 —What did I say?
    That he made chairs, and was a joiner and carpenter.
    —I said he made chairs, but I did not say he was a carpenter.
    All right then, he's just an amateur.
    —Perhaps! Would you say a thrush was a professional flautist, or
      just an amateur?—
20 I'd say it was just a bird.
    —And I say he is just a man.
    All right! You always did quibble.

Spray

It is a wonder foam is so beautiful.
A wave bursts in anger on a rock, broken up
in wild white sibilant spray
and falls back, drawing in its breath with rage,
with frustration how beautiful!

Sea-Weed

This poem was first published in **Dial** in July 1929.

> What techniques or devices does Lawrence employ in this poem to portray the movement of the sea-weed?

> How does the mood in Sea-Weed match the mood of Spray?

Many Mansions

> How can this poem be related to A Living?

Poverty

Here again is some social comment articulating Lawrence's critical view of the rich in society. At the same time, he affirms his own claim to be working-class.

1   *My Lady Poverty* – an allegorical character, who embodies certain qualities (e.g. holiness, humility) associated with being poor – though not generally, it must be said, by the poor themselves, as Lawrence implies.

3   *Saint Francis* – founder of the Christian Franciscan religious order of friars. He was the son of a wealthy cloth merchant but took to a life of poverty instead of pleasure.

Sea-Weed

Sea-weed sways and sways and swirls
as if swaying were its form of stillness;
and if it flushes against fierce rock
it slips over it as shadows do, without hurting itself.

Many Mansions

When a bird flips his tail in getting his balance on a tree
he feels much gayer than if somebody had left him a fortune
or than if he'd just built himself a nest with a bathroom—
Why can't people be gay like that?

Poverty

The only people I ever heard talk about My Lady Poverty
were rich people, or people who imagined themselves rich.
Saint Francis himself was a rich and spoiled young man.

Being born among the working people
5 I know that poverty is a hard old hag,
and a monster, when you're pinched for actual necessities.
And whoever says she isn't, is a liar.

I don't want to be poor, it means I am pinched.
But neither do I want to be rich.
10 When I look at this pine-tree near the sea,
that grows out of rock, and plumes forth, plumes forth,
I see it has a natural abundance.

Why is the air 'full of wine' (line 15)?

What is Lawrence really implying in his jocular use of 'My Lady Poverty'?

Talk

3   *draughts* – literally, intrusive currents of cold air.

Are the people talking directly to Lawrence or possibly intruding on his calm and collected thoughts by talking behind him?

Consider what Lawrence means by the 'draughts' that leave him cold inside.

Can't Be Borne

How does the title of this poem relate to the cutting opinion expressed? Does its attitude contradict Lawrence's view of love, sex and relationships expressed elsewhere?

Are there any ways in which you find this poem hackneyed or unoriginal? Is it too much of a cliché to be worth publishing?

After All the Tragedies Are Over –

2   *Hamlet* – The eponymous tragic hero of Shakespeare's play.

With its roots it has a grand grip on its daily bread,
and its plumes look like green cups held up to the sun and air
15   and full of wine.

I want to be like that, to have a natural abundance
and plume forth, and be splendid.

Talk

I wish people, when you sit near them,
wouldn't think it necessary to make conversation
and send thin draughts of words
blowing down your neck and your ears
and giving you a cold in your inside.

Can't Be Borne

Any woman who says to me
—Do you really love me?—
earns my undying detestation.

After All the Tragedies Are Over—

After all the tragedies are over and worn out
and a man can no longer feel heroic about being a Hamlet—
When love is gone, and desire is dead, and tragedy has left the heart
then grief and pain go too, withdrawing
5   from the heart and leaving strange cold stretches of sand.

10   *nonetity* – an unimportant or non-existent thing or person.

19   *denuding* – stripping bare or naked.

If read aloud, how does the rhythm of the poem direct you towards the key phrases in it?

Does the imagery of the sea and coast help you to understand Lawrence's view of the tide of life?

Is this an optimistic or a pessimistic poem?

The Optimist

What is the essence of this 'thought'?

How does the tone of the poem complement or contrast with After All the Tragedies are Over?

So a man no longer knows his own heart;
he might say into the twilight: What is it?
I am here, yet my heart is bare and utterly empty.
I have passed from existence, I feel nothing any more.
10 I am a nonentity.—

Yet, when the time has come to be nothing, how good it is to be
    nothing!
a waste expanse of nothing, like wide foreshores where not a
    ripple is left
15 and the sea is lost
in the lapse of the lowest of tides.

Ah, when I have seen myself left by life, left nothing!

Yet even waste, grey foreshores, sand, and sorry, far-out clay
are sea-bed still, through their hour of bare denuding
20 It is the moon that turns the tides.
The beaches can do nothing about it.

The Optimist

The optimist builds himself safe inside a cell
and paints the inside walls sky-blue
and blocks up the door
and says he's in heaven.

Lizard

3   *dandy* – a now obsolete colloquialism (a word used in common or everyday speech) for splendid or excellent; also a man obsessively devoted to smartness, mannerisms and fashion.

> Do both meanings of 'dandy' apply in this poem?

Censors

In this poem Lawrence clearly gives vent to his frustration with the authorities in England over the censorship of his work (see page 106).

9   *stertorous* – apparent snoring and blocked heavy breathing caused by an obstruction.

> Why might censors have a 'stern eye on life'?

> Suggest why the poet introduces and closes line 7 with a dash.

> Does the death imagery clearly reveal the differences between the 'sunny man' and the censors?

Now It's Happened

This poem – showing a return to rhyme and recognizable form – voices Lawrence's disillusion with the progress of the Russian Revolution.

3   *Vronsky and Anna* – the lovers in the Tolstoy novel *Anna Karenina* (1865-9). In the story, the unhappily married heroine leaves her repressive husband and elopes with Vronsky, whom she loves. However, the lovers never achieve liberation and Anna is driven by despair to commit suicide.

Lizard

A lizard ran out on a rock and looked up, listening
no doubt to the sounding of the spheres.
And what a dandy fellow! the right toss of a chin for you
and swirl of a tail!

5   If men were as much men as lizards are lizards
they'd be worth looking at.

Censors

Censors are dead men
set up to judge between life and death.
For no live, sunny man would be a censor,
he'd just laugh.

5   But censors, being dead men,
have a stern eye on life.
—That thing's alive! It's dangerous. Make away
with it!—
And when the execution is performed
10   you hear the stertorous, self-righteous heavy breathing of the dead
      men,
the censors, breathing with relief.

Now It's Happened

One cannot now help thinking
how much better it would have been
if Vronsky and Anna Karenin
had stood up for themselves, and seen

6   Lenin – founder of the Bolsheviks and leader of the 1917 October Revolution. He headed the first Soviet government but in 1921, after the Civil War, he adopted the New Economic Policy which virtually ruined the economy. He died in 1924.

11   *Dostoevsky and Tchekov* – Dostoevsky was a novelist who explored the darker side of the human spirit and the suffering of ordinary people in Tsarist Russia. As a result of his beliefs and revolutionary interests he was sent to a labour camp in Siberia. Tchekov was a nineteenth-century playwright who indirectly criticized the decline of rural, middle-class Russia in his plays.

12   *spy-government* – both before and after the Revolution, a vast network of spies bolstered the governments and set citizen against citizen.

13   *Tolstoi* – A Russian aristocrat and novelist who in later life became concerned with social problems and adopted a form of Christianity based on non-resistance to evil. He was regarded by many Russians as a saint and moral teacher. As a Count, he freed his own peasants from the old Russian system of service called serfdom before the Tsar abolished it in 1861. Tolstoi died a very old man in 1910.

24   *Russian nobility* – the aristocrats and royal family felt that it was their right and duty to rule and protect the peasants in pre-revolutionary Russia.

28   *sob-stuff crown* – alluding to a saintly crown or halo and the reverence or divinity wrongly attributed to leaders.

29   *tenets* – doctrines or beliefs held by a group.

31   *Willy wet-leg* – a colloquial figure of speech implying self-pity and cowardice.

What other things do you need to know before fully understanding this poem?

Is the title of this poem ironic?

Do the colloquialisms in lines 28, 31 and 32 enhance Lawrence's argument or trivialize his point?

5   Russia across her crisis,
    instead of leaving it to Lenin.

    The big, flamboyant Russia
    might have been saved, if a pair
    of rebels like Anna and Vronsky
10 had blasted the sickly air
    of Dostoevsky and Tchekov,
    and spy-government everywhere.

    But Tolstoi was a traitor
    to the Russia that need him most,
15 the clumsy, bewildered Russia
    so worried by the Holy Ghost.
    He shifted his job on to the peasants
    and landed them all on toast.

    Dostoevsky, the Judas,
20 with his sham christianity
    epileptically ruined
    the last bit of sanity
    left in the hefty bodies
    of the Russian nobility.

25 So our goody-good men betray us
    and our sainty-saints let us down,
    and a sickly people will slay us
    if we touch the sob-stuff crown
    of such martyrs; while Marxian tenets
30 naturally take hold of the town.

    Too much of the humble Willy wet-leg
    and the holy can't-help-it touch,
    till you've ruined a nation's fibre
    and they loathe all feeling as such,
35 and want to be cold and devilish hard
    like machines—and you can't wonder much.—

Intimates

This stinging 'thought' smacks of personal experience and bitterness.

> What phrases hint at the nature of the woman's narcissism (extreme self-love)?

> How does the short, sharp ending convey the narrator's haste and maybe the balance of power between the couple? Is the poem self-mocking? Is it really poetry?

Trees in the Garden

7   *evanescent* – passing away or vanishing.
7   *variegated* – marked with different colours or patches.

Intimates

Don't you care for my love? she said bitterly.

I handed her the mirror, and said:
Please address these questions to the proper person!
Please make all requests to head-quarters!
5 In all matters of emotional importance
please approach the supreme authority direct!—
So I handed her the mirror.

And she would have broken it over my head,
but she caught sight of her own reflection
10 and that held her spellbound for two seconds
while I fled.

Trees in the Garden

Ah in the thunder air
how still the trees are!

And the lime-tree, lovely and tall, every leaf silent
hardly looses even a last breath of perfume.

5 And the ghostly, creamy coloured little trees of leaves
white, ivory white among the rambling greens
how evanescent, variegated elder, she hesitates on the green grass
as if, in another moment, she would disappear
with all her grace of foam!

On a first reading, what strikes you as familiar about the poem?

What is the association between the trees and the sea in the poem?

From *Last Poems*

Many of Lawrence's last poems use the ancient myths of the Mediterranean gods, who presided over human affairs, to explore the meaning of death. By this time, Lawrence was living in the south of France and in the last year of his life.

The Greeks Are Coming

2 *furl* – the act of rolling up tightly.

5 *Cnossos* – an alternative spelling of Knossos, the ruined city in central Crete and the centre of the ancient Mediterranean Minoan civilization. Minos, the son of Zeus, was the ruler of Crete and founder of the Bronze Age Minoan civilization which worshipped a great white bull, a symbol of fertility. Cretans had a reputation for being warlike and great seamen or pirates.

6 *Aegean* – the area around the Aegean sea and islands and/or the ancient civilization of the area.

What might be significant about the 'morning end of the sea' and this stage in the poet's life?

What conclusion is Lawrence drawing by contrasting the ancient ships of Cnossos with the modern liner?

The Argonauts

The Argonauts, led by Jason, set sail on a quest for the Golden Fleece of the Winged Ram. They had many adventures and visited new lands.

10   And the larch that is only a column, it goes up too tall to see:
And the balsam-pines that are blue with the grey-blue blueness of
things from the sea,
And the young copper beech, its leaves red-rosy at the ends
how still they are together, they stand so still
15   in the thunder air, all strangers to one another
as the green grass glows upwards, strangers in the garden.

Lichtental

Later Poems

The Greeks Are Coming!

Little islands out at sea, on the horizon
keep suddenly showing a whiteness, a flash and a furl, a hail
of something coming, ships a-sail from over the rim of the sea.

And every time, it is ships, it is ships,
5   it is ships of Cnossos coming, out of the morning end of the sea,
it is Aegean ships, and men with archaic pointed beards
coming out of the eastern end.

But it is far-off foam.
And an ocean liner, going east, like a small beetle walking the edge
10   is leaving a long thread of dark smoke
like a bad smell.

The Argonauts

They are not dead, they are not dead!
Now that the sun, like a lion, licks his paws
and goes slowly down the hill:

5 *crescent* – a curved shape like that of a half-moon. Here the moon, ascends as the hostile lion-pawed sun sinks.

9 *Odysseus* – hero of the siege of Troy and noted for his strength. After the fall of Troy, he wandered the seas for ten years, having many adventures, before returning to his homeland. His Roman name was Ulysses.

10 *pain-grillé* – toasted bread (French).

What different times of day are described in the poem?

What is your reaction to the hint of everyday life in line 10? Does it add a personal context to the poem?

Middle of the World

The centre of the ancient western world and the cradle of its civilization was the Mediterranean Sea, hence the title of the poem.

4 *Dionysos* – the Greek god of wine, cultivation and fertility. His final feat was to change himself into a lion, the ship's mast into a tree with vines and the sailors into dolphins. His Roman name was Bacchus. (See notes on *Peace* and *The Argonauts*.)

7 *P. & O. and the Orient Line* – two large ocean liner companies in the early part of the twentieth century.

8 *Minoan distance* – the sea between Greece and Crete, formerly ruled by King Minos.

11 *exaltation* – the act of praising or excitement and elation.

13 *archaic smile* – the name given to the faint, mysterious smile on the faces of early Greek statues.

now that the moon, who remembers, and only cares
5 that we should be lovely in the flesh, with bright, crescent feet,
pauses near the crest of the hill, climbing slowly, like a queen
looking down on the lion as he retreats—

Now the sea is the Argonauts' sea, and in the dawn
Odysseus calls the commands, as he steers past those foamy islands;
10 wait, wait, don't bring the coffee yet, nor the *pain grillé.*
The dawn is not off the sea, and Odysseus' ships
have not yet passed the islands, I must watch them still.

Middle of the World

This sea will never die, neither will it ever grow old
nor cease to be blue, nor in the dawn
cease to lift up its hills
and let the slim black ship of Dionysos come sailing in
5 with grape-vines up the mast, and dolphins leaping.

What do I care if the smoking ships
of the P. & O. and the Orient Line and all the other stinkers
cross like clock-work the Minoan distance!
They only cross, the distance never changes.

10 And now that the moon who gives men glistening bodies
is in her exaltation, and can look down on the sun
I see descending from the ships at dawn
slim naked men from Cnossos, smiling the archaic smile
of those that will without fail come back again,
15 and kindling little fires upon the shores
and crouching, and speaking the music of lost languages.

17 *Tiryns* – this was an important Greek city-state in the Bronze Age, with its own gods.

They Say the Sea is Loveless

How does this poem convey the sensuality of the sea?

What associations can be made between the ideas in this poem and those expressed in Middle of the World? Which poem extends these ideas furthest?

Butterfly

7 *geraniums* – a flowering plant common in the Mediterranean.

And the Minoan Gods, and the Gods of Tiryns
are heard softly laughing and chatting, as ever;
and Dionysos, young, and a stranger
20 leans listening on the gate, in all respect.

They Say the Sea is Loveless

They say the sea is loveless, that in the sea
love cannot live, but only bare, salt splinters
of loveless life.

But from the sea
5 the dolphins leap round Dionysos' ship
whose masts have purple vines,
and up they come with the purple dark of rainbows
and flip! they go! with the nose-dive of sheer delight;
and the sea is making love to Dionysos
10 in the bouncing of these small and happy whales.

Butterfly

Butterfly, the wind blows sea-ward, strong beyond the garden wall!
Butterfly, why do you settle on my shoe, and sip the dirt on my shoe,
Lifting your veined wings, lifting them? big white butterfly!

Already it is October, and the wind blows strong to the sea
5 from the hills where snow must have fallen, the wind is polished
    with snow.
Here in the garden, with red geraniums, it is warm, it is warm
but the wind blows strong to sea-ward, white butterfly, content on
    my shoe!

14 *arch-crest* – this is the highest point from which the butterfly moves or is forced into another direction.

How can the wind be polished with snow?

What is the significance of the fact that the insect is being buffeted and then blown seaward? How does Lawrence's observation of the butterfly become visionary and reveal the underlying meaning of the poem?

Bavarian Gentians

This poem was written in September 1929. Gentians are mountain plants with deep blue flowers. An earlier, shorter version of the poem was called *Glory of Darkness* and was then redrafted and retitled. There are two versions entitled *Bavarian Gentians* appearing consecutively in a notebook found after Lawrence's death. The poems differ in crucial respects and it is not definitely known which was the final draft.

2   *Michaelmas* – the feast of St Michael on 29 September and so associated with Autumn.

5   *Pluto* – in Greek mythology he was the god of Hades, the underworld, and brother of Zeus and Poseidon. He was called Dis by the Romans.

10 *Demeter* – the Greek goddess of agricultural fertility and mother of Persephone.

17 *Persephone* – daughter of Zeus and Demeter, who was abducted by Pluto and forced to marry him but was eventually allowed to visit the living world for part of each year. While Demeter searched for Persephone, the land became uncultivated and winter appeared. When Persephone returned for half the year, summer returned with her.

Where do you think the stairs in line 15 lead to?

What is the paradox in Lawrence's description of the gentians as flowers 'giving off darkness'?

10   Will you go, will you go from my warm house?
       Will you climb on your big soft wings, black-dotted,
       as up an invisible rainbow, an arch
       till the wind slides you sheer from the arch-crest
       and in a strange level fluttering you go out to sea-ward, white speck!

15   Farewell, farewell, lost soul!
       you have melted in the crystalline distance,
       it is enough! I saw you vanish into air.

Bavarian Gentians

       Not every man has gentians in his house
       in Soft September, at slow, sad Michaelmas.

       Bavarian gentians, big and dark, only dark
       darkening the day-time, torch-like with the smoking blueness of
           Pluto's gloom,
5   ribbed and torch-like, with their blaze of darkness spread blue
       down flattening into points, flattened under the sweep of white day
       torch-flower of the blue-smoking darkness, Pluto's dark-blue daze,
       black lamps from the halls of Dis, burning dark blue,
10   giving off darkness, blue darkness, as Demeter's pale lamps give off
           light,
       lead me then, lead the way.

       Reach me a gentian, give me a torch!
       let me guide myself with the blue, forked torch of this flower
15   down the darker and darker stairs, where blue is darkened on
           blueness
       even where Persephone goes, just now, from the frosted September
       to the sightless realm where darkness is awake upon the dark
       and Persephone herself is but a voice

How is the poem similar to an incantation – a recitation of words or sounds for magical purposes?

Does the poem leave you with a sense of the possibility of renewal in death? Or does it leave you with a sense of inevitable gloom? Why?

In the Cities

3   *benzine* – used as a solvent in petrol.

6   *miasma* – a swamp mist or the odour of corruption.

9   *insolent* – insulting.

12 *litter-bearers* – the servants or (in Ancient Rome) slaves who carried a litter, a form of transport consisting of a chair or couch supported by poles, like a stretcher.

13 *Mycenae* – a Bronze Age city-state in the Peloponnese, the Kingdom of Agamemnon. The Lion Gate still survives in the ruins of the city.

19 *bursten* – the archaic past participle of to burst open, like a swelling or boil.

21 *mire* – a swamp or boggy ground.

Is the sparse punctuation in the first two stanzas confusing? What is Lawrence trying to evoke in this opening section of the poem?

What is Lawrence suggesting in this poem about the way the past relates to the present?

How does Lawrence contrast the filth of modern cities with the splendour of the cities of antiquity?

or a darkness invisible enfolded in the deeper dark
20   of the arms Plutonic, and pierced with the passion of dense gloom,
among the splendour of torches of darkness, shedding darkness on
the lost bride and her groom.

In the Cities

In the cities
there is even no more any weather
the weather in town is always benzine, or else petrol fumes
lubricating oil, exhaust gas.

5   As over some dense marsh, the fumes
thicken, miasma, the fumes of the automobile
densely thicken in the cities.

In ancient Rome, down the thronged streets
no wheels might run, no insolent chariots.
10   Only the footsteps, footsteps
of people
and the gentle trotting of the litter-bearers.

In Minos, in Mycenae
in all the cities with lion gates
15   the dead threaded the air, lingering
lingering in the earth's shadow
and leaning towards the old hearth.

In London, New York, Paris
in the bursten cities
20   the dead tread heavily through the muddy air
through the mire of fumes
heavily, stepping weary on our hearts.

Mana of the Sea

Mana means supernatural or magic power.

9   *islets* – small islands.

What might the poet have meant by 'the tide in my arms' (line 4)?

Why do you think the poem is set out as a series of questions?

Mystic

4   *welter* – a rolling movement, a state of chaos or confusion.

Mana of the Sea

Do you see the sea, breaking itself to bits against the islands
yet remaining unbroken, the level great sea?

Have I caught from it
the tide in my arms
5   that runs down to the shallows of my wrists, and breaks
abroad in my hands, like waves among the rocks of substance?

Do the rollers of the sea
roll down my thighs
and over the submerged islets of my knees
10 with power, sea-power
sea-power
to break against the ground
in the flat, recurrent breakers of my two feet?

And is my body ocean, ocean
15 whose power runs to the shores along my arms
and breaks in the foamy hands, whose power rolls out
to the white-treading waves of two salt feet?

I am the sea, I am the sea!

Mystic

They call all experience of the senses *mystic*, when the experience is
   considered.
So an apple becomes *mystic* when I taste in it
the summer and the snows, the wild welter of earth
5 and the insistence of the sun.

7   *preponderantly* – for the most part, mainly.

8   *brackish* – slightly salty.

> What phrases describe the qualities of the apple the poet broods over? Does he have an affinity with the fruit?

> In what ways does this poem summarize Lawrence's approach to his writings and also towards life as a whole?

Anaxagoras

Anaxagoras (500-428 BC) was a Greek philosopher who taught that all things are made up of particles arranged by a external intelligence. He also extended his theory to say that all particles contain every single type of particle in them. For example, hot also contains an element of cold and black must have a small element of white in it.

3   *enunciating* – stating, giving voice to.

14   *ominousness* – threat or foreboding.

All of which things I can surely taste in a good apple.
Though some apples taste preponderantly of water, wet and sour
and some of too much sun, brackish sweet
like lagoon-water, that has been too much sunned.

10 If I say I taste these things in an apple, I am called *mystic*, which
  means a liar.
The only way to eat an apple is to hog it down like a pig
and taste nothing
that is *real*.

15 But if I eat an apple, I like to eat it with all my senses awake.
Hogging it down like a pig I call the feeding of corpses.

Anaxagoras

When Anaxagoras says: Even the snow is black!
he is taken by the scientists very seriously
because he is enunciating a 'principle', a 'law'
that all things are mixed, and therefore the purest white snow
5 has in it an element of blackness.

That they call science, and reality.
I call it mental conceit and mystification
and nonsense, for pure snow is white to us
white and white and only white
10 with a lovely bloom of whiteness upon white
in which the soul delights and the senses
have an experience of bliss.

And life is for delight, and for bliss
and dread, and the dark, rolling ominousness of doom
15 then the bright dawning of delight again
from off the sheer white snow, or the poised moon.

18   *scylla* – a small blue spring flower of the hyacinth family.

> *In what ways does Lawrence's passionate apprehension of the physical world conflict with the philosophical theories of Anaxagora?*

Death is Not Evil, Evil is Mechanical

This complicated poem appears at first to be confusing and contradictory. Lawrence wrote in 1929: 'There is an evil world-soul, which sometimes overpowers one, and which one has to struggle most of the time to keep oneself clear.'

1   *absolved* – released or pardoned from obligation, blame or sin.

3   *ego* – the 'self' of an individual. In Freudian psychology, the ego, the conscious mind, controls anti-social behaviour.

7   *Dante* – the Italian poet (1265–1321) who wrote *The Divine Comedy*, an allegorical account of his passage through Hell, Purgatory and Paradise, which was a journey of moral and spirtual enlightenment.

9   *Know thyself* – this is the inscription on the temple of Apollo – in Greek mythology, god of light, poetry, music, healing and prophecy – at Delphi, the ancient Greek shrine. To the ancient Greeks, these words summed up the conflict between the emotional or instinctive and the rational elements in the human spirit.

19   *cataract* – a torrent or waterfall.

> *What is the central image of the first stanza? How does this contrast with the ideas in the last stanza?*

> *How do Lawrence's views on the effect of the 'evil world-soul' illuminate the ideas in this poem?*

And in the shadow of the sun the snow is blue, so blue-aloof
with a hint of the frozen bells of the scylla flower
but never the ghost of a glimpse of Anaxagoras' funeral black.

Death is Not Evil, Evil is Mechanical

Only the human being, absolved from kissing and strife
goes on and on and on, without wandering
fixed upon the hub of the ego
going, yet never wandering, fixed, yet in motion,
5 the kind of hell that is real, grey and awful
sinless and stainless going round and round
the kind of hell grey Dante never saw
but of which he had a bit inside him.

Know thyself, and that thou art mortal.
10 But know thyself, denying that thou art mortal:
a thing of kisses and strife
a lit-up shaft of rain
a calling column of blood
a rose tree bronzey with thorns
15 a mixture of yea and nay
a rainbow of love and hate
a wind that blows back and forth
a creature of beautiful peace, like a river
and a creature of conflict, like a cataract:
20 know thyself, in denial of all these things—

And thou shalt begin to spin round on the hub of the obscene ego
a grey void thing that goes without wandering
a machine that in itself is nothing
a centre of the evil world.

The Ship of Death

This poem, like *Bavarian Gentians*, is a meditation on the soul and death as the prelude to renewal, and a search for unknown knowledge. Here the soul travels towards death and Lawrence takes as the central concept of the poem the ancient Egyptian religious belief that the soul was carried to the Land of the Dead by ship. Another clue to this poem and the use of 'oblivion' in *Shadows* is mentioned in his travel book **Etruscan Places**, published in 1932. In chapter 1 he writes that in this ancient pre-Roman culture of northern Italy, death was thought of as neither blissful nor purgatorial but rather as a natural continuation of life.

2   *oblivion* – the state of having (or being) forgotten; unknowingness.

8   *ship of death* – in ancient Egyptian religion, the soul of a person was carried by ship from the East, the land of the living, over to the West, the land of the dead. The Etruscans placed a small bronze ship in the tombs of their chiefs.

16   *orifices* – openings or holes.

17   *quietus* – a release from life, and so death or a settlement of doubt.

17-23   *And can a man...ever a quietus make* – this echoes Shakespeare's *Hamlet* 3,i, where the prince asks what reason there is to endure the pain of life when suicide offers the prospect of early release.

Explain what has bruised the body and frightened the soul in section II.

The Ship of Death

I

Now it is autumn and the falling fruit
and the long journey towards oblivion.

The apples falling like great drops of dew
to bruise themselves an exit from themselves.

5 And it is time to go, to bid farewell
to one's own self, and find an exit
from the fallen self.

II

Have you built your ship of death, O have you?
O build your ship of death, for you will need it.

10 The grim frost is at hand, when the apples will fall
thick, almost thundrous, on the hardened earth.

And death is on the air like a smell of ashes!
Ah! can't you smell it?

And in the bruised body, the frightened soul
15 finds itself shrinking, wincing from the cold
that blows upon it through the orifices.

III

And can a man his own quietus make
with a bare bodkin?

With daggers, bodkins, bullets, man can make
20 a bruise or break of exit for his life;
but is that a quietus, O tell me, is it quietus?

36   *breaches* – gaps or holes in fortifications or defensive walls.

What typical Lawrentian techniques can you identify in this poem?

Does Lawrence associate himself with any particular religious doctrine in this poem?

Does the digression on Hamlet and suicide add to or detract from the strength of the poem as a whole? Does Lawrence reject suicide?

Surely not so! for how could murder, even self-murder
ever a quietus make?

IV
O let us talk of quiet that we know,
25 that we can know, the deep and lovely quiet
of a strong heart at peace!

How can we this, our own quietus, make?

V
Build then the ship of death, for you must take
the longest journey, to oblivion.

30 And die the death, the long and painful death
that lies between the old self and the new.

Already our bodies are fallen, bruised, badly bruised,
already our souls are oozing through the exit
of the cruel bruise.

35 Already the dark and endless ocean of the end
is washing in through the breaches of our wounds,
already the flood is upon us.

Oh build your ship of death, your little ark
and furnish it with food, with little cakes, and wine
40 for the dark flight down oblivion.

VI
Piecemeal the body dies, and the timid soul
has her footing washed away, as the dark flood rises.

We are dying, we are dying, we are all of us dying
and nothing will stay the death-flood rising within us
45 and soon it will rise on the world, on the outside world.

48   *cowers* – crouches, shrinks away from (something feared).

54   *accoutrements* – formal trappings, clothing or equipment.

We are dying, we are dying, piecemeal our bodies are dying
and our strength leaves us,
and our soul cowers naked in the dark rain over the flood,
cowering in the last branches of the tree of our life.

VII

50 We are dying, we are dying, so all we can do
is now to be willing to die, and to build the ship
of death to carry the soul on the longest journey.

A little ship, with oars and food
and little dishes, and all accoutrements
55 fitting and ready for the departing soul.

Now launch the small ship, now as the body dies
and life departs, launch out, the fragile soul
in the fragile ship of courage, the ark of faith
with its store of food and little cooking pans
60 and change of clothes,
upon the flood's black waste
upon the waters of the end
upon the sea of death, where still we sail
darkly, for we cannot steer, and have no port.

65 There is no port, there is nowhere to go
only the deepening blackness darkening still
blacker upon the soundless, ungurgling flood
darkness at one with darkness, up and down
and sideways utterly dark, so there is no direction any more.
70 and the little ship is there; yet she is gone.
She is not seen, for there is nothing to see her by.
She is gone! gone! and yet
somewhere she is there.
Nowhere!

95   *wan* – pale or sickly.

VIII

75 And everything is gone, the body is gone
completely under, gone, entirely gone.
The upper darkness is heavy as the lower,
between them the little ship
is gone
80 she is gone.

It is the end, it is oblivion.

IX
And yet out of eternity, a thread
separates itself on the blackness,
a horizontal thread
85 that fumes a little with pallor upon the dark.

Is it illusion? or does the pallor fume
A little higher?
Ah wait, wait, for there's the dawn,
the cruel dawn of coming back to life
90 out of oblivion.

Wait, wait, the little ship
drifting, beneath the deathly ashy grey
of a flood-dawn.

Wait, wait! even so, a flush of yellow
95 and strangely, O chilled wan soul, a flush of rose.

A flush of rose, and the whole thing starts again.

X
The flood subsides, and the body, like a worn sea-shell
emerges strange and lovely.
And the little ship wings home, faltering and lapsing
100 on the pink flood.
and the frail soul steps out, into her house again
filling the heart with peace.

What does the phrase 'soundless, ungurgling flood' (line 67) evoke?

Is there a sense of resurrection or afterlife in this poem?

All Souls' Day

All Souls' Day is 2 November (see *Giorni Dei Morti*, page 59). In some predominantly Roman Catholic cultures, it is customary for families to visit the graves of their deceased relatives on this day and leave gifts of food and flowers on the tombs.

9   *conical* – cone-shaped.

16 *proper store of meal* – in their tombs, the Egyptians provided not only ships for the journey to the Land of the Dead but also food and everything the soul might need on its passage.

What is the mood of this poem?

Lawrence refers in line 16 to the Egyptian practice but, in the last stanza, where is he suggesting that the 'soul-food' might come from?

Swings the heart renewed with peace
even of oblivion.

105 Oh build your ship of death, oh build it!
for you will need it.
For the voyage of oblivion awaits you.

All Souls' Day

Be careful, then, and be gentle about death.
For it is hard to die, it is difficult to go through
the door, even when it opens.

And the poor dead, when they have left the walled
5 and silvery city of the now hopeless body
where are they to go, Oh where are they to go?

They linger in the shadow of the earth.
The earth's long conical shadow is full of souls
that cannot find the way across the sea of change.

10 Be kind, Oh be kind to your dead
and give them a little encouragement
and help them to build their little ship of death.

For the soul has a long, long journey after death
to the sweet home of pure oblivion.
15 Each needs a little ship, a little ship
and the proper store of meal for the longest journey.

Oh, from out of your heart
provide for your dead once more, equip them
like departing mariners, lovingly.

15   *drowse* – half-asleep state.

16   *Singing darker than the nightingale* – there is a slight echo of or allusion to Keat's *Ode to a Nightingale* here. In Keats' poem the poet (who, like Lawrence, was mortally ill) is weighed down by the misery of the world and seems to desire oblivion.

16   *solstice* – the two points in the cycle of the earth around the sun when the sun is farthest away from the earth's equator, i.e. either 21 June or 22 December, the longest and shortest days of the year respectively in the northern hemisphere.

How does the technique of repeating 'And if' help you to become aware of Lawrence's feelings of apprehension?

How is this poem different in its use of the pattern and movement of imagery from his other deliberations on death?

Shadows

And if tonight my soul may find her peace
in sleep, and sink in good oblivion,
and in the morning wake like a new-opened flower
then I have been dipped again in God, and new-created.
5 And if, as weeks go round, in the dark of the moon
my spirit darkens and goes out, and soft strange gloom
pervades my movements and my thoughts and words
then I shall know that I am walking still
with God, we are close together together now the moon's in shadow.

10 And if, as autumn deepens and darkens
I feel the pain of falling leaves, and stems that break in storms
and trouble and dissolution and distress
and then the softness of deep shadows folding, folding
around my soul and spirit, around my lips
15 so sweet, like a swoon, or more like the drowse of a low, sad song
singing darker than the nightingale, on, on to the solstice
and the silence of short days, the silence of the year, the shadow,
then I shall know that my life is moving still
with the dark earth, and drenched
20 with the deep oblivion of earth's lapse and renewal.

And if, in the changing phases of man's life
I fall in sickness and in misery
my wrists seem broken and my heart seems dead
and strength is gone, and my life
25 is only the leavings of a life:

and still, among it all, snatches of lovely oblivion, and snatches of
  renewal
odd, wintry flowers upon the withered stem, yet new, strange flowers
such as my life has not brought forth before, new blossoms of me—

We Have Gone Too Far

9   *serried* – an archaic word meaning 'pressed together', used particularly of ranks of soldiers.

20   *To lap* – to wrap up, enfold in a protective environment.
21   *immemorial* – originating in the distant past; timeless.

30   then I must know that still
        I am in the hands [of] the unknown God,
        he is breaking me down to his own oblivion
        to send me forth on a new morning, a new man.

We Have Gone Too Far

We have gone too far, oh very much too far,
Only attend to the noiseless multitudes
Of ghosts that throng about our muffled hearts.

Only behold the ghosts, the ghosts of the slain,
5 Behold them homeless and houseless, without complaint
Of their patient waiting upon us, the throng of the ghosts.

And say, what matters any more, what matters,
Save the cold ghosts that homeless flock about
Our serried hearts, drifting without a place?

10 What matters any more, but only love?
There's only love that matters any more.
There's only love, the rest is all outspent.

Let us receive our ghosts and give them place,
Open the ranks, and let them in our hearts,
15 And lay them deep in love, lay them to sleep.

The foe can take our goods, our homes and land,
Also the lives that still he may require,
But leave us still to love, still leave us love.

Leave us to take our ghosts into our hearts,
20 To lap them round with love, and lay them by
To sleep at last in immemorial love.

30 *gossamer* – a filmy cobweb or gauze.

30 *prevalent* – widespread or common.

35 *twilight of the Gods* – the Götterdämmerung of Germanic myth, the end of the world and the destruction of the gods.

36 *Hesperides* – in Greek myth, the four daughters of Atlas and Hesperis, who lived in the garden of the gods at the end of the world and guarded the tree with the golden apples which the earth-goddess Gaea had caused to grow as a wedding present for Hera, wife of Zeus. Heracles stole the apples but they were eventually returned.

40 *vaunt* – boast.

Who might be the 'foe' in line 16?

In what other poems does the colour 'grey', line 34, appear? Does its symbolism here resemble that in the other poems in which it is used?

What point is Lawrence making when he re-uses 'serried' with 'prevalent' in line 32?

We let the weapons slip from out our hands,
We loose our grip, and we unstrain our eyes,
We let our souls be pure and vulnerable.

25   We cover the houseless dead, so they sleep in peace,
We yield the enemy his last demands,
So he too may be healed, be soothed to peace.

For now the hosts of homeless ghosts do throng
To many about us, so we wander about
30   Blind with the gossamer of prevalent death.
But let us free our eyes, and look beyond
This serried ecstasy of prevalent death,
And pass beyond, with the foe and the homeless ghosts.

Let us rise up, and go from out this grey
35   Last twilight of the Gods, to find again
The lost Hesperides where love is pure.

For we have gone too far, oh much too far
Towards the darkness and the shadow of death;
Let us turn back, lest we should all be lost.

40   Let us go back now, though we give up all
The treasure and the vaunt we ever had,
Let us go back, the only way is love.

CRITICAL APPROACHES

Lawrence's poetry can be approached from a variety of standpoints or theories. You will gain a deeper understanding of the meaning of the poems by looking at them in terms of Lawrence's life, work and the literary times he lived in. An understanding of the form, style and use of language in a poet's work is also vital to your reading of the poems. Lawrence had a lot to say about form and technique in poetry. He was an innovator and at the forefront of many of the changes in modern verse. The sections in Critical Approaches will help you to understand Lawrence's poetry more fully.

Remember that you bring your own knowledge of language, cultural background and ideas to your reading of the poems.

Lawrence's life

D.H. Lawrence was born on 11 September 1885 in the Nottinghamshire mining village of Eastwood. His father, Arthur Lawrence, was a miner, and his mother was an intelligent woman who had educational and social aspirations for her children. Not surprisingly there was a great deal of bitterness and antagonism between the two. The forceful and possessive Mrs Lawrence had an increasing hold over her son, who was well aware of his mother's expectations and later spent much of his early adulthood releasing himself from her influence.

He was a sensitive, gifted and intelligent child. In 1901, he became seriously ill with a bout of pneumonia that seriously affected his lungs. For the rest of his life he suffered from periods of illness and was eventually diagnosed as suffering from tuberculosis in 1925.

In 1898, Lawrence won a scholarship to Nottingham High School. By 1903 he was attending a part-time teacher-training course. During this time he read widely and also began to discuss and formulate his ideas on politics and philosophy.

By 1905, he had composed his first poems and in 1906 was drafting his first novel, *The White Peacock*. In the same year he started to work for his teacher's certificate at Nottingham University College. For some years he had known a local girl called Jessie Chambers, with whom he had struck up an intense friendship. Although it seems that the relationship did not develop sexually until 1910, she exerted a great influence on him until 1912.

In 1908, Lawrence was offered the chance to teach in Croydon. Two years later, his mother died. He became ill at the end of 1911, and decided to abandon teaching. He planned to go to Germany and, while visiting Professor Ernest Weekley for advice, he first met the professor's wife, Frieda, who was German. She and Weekley had three children but Frieda and Lawrence fell in love. This very unconventional pair, whose relationship was often turbulent, left for Germany. The next few years were one of Lawrence's most productive periods but the couple returned to England and married in the summer of 1914. During 1916–17 they lived in Cornwall, but because of Frieda's German background they were suspected of being spies and were forced to leave. Lawrence's novel *The Rainbow*, published in 1915, was also banned as obscene because of its portrayal of sexual relationships between men and women.

Between 1919 and 1922 the Lawrences visited various parts of Italy and Germany. In 1920 the novel *Women in Love* was published.

The couple left for Ceylon (Sri Lanka) and Australia, where *Kangaroo*, published in 1923, was set. Further expeditions took the Lawrences to New Zealand, Tahiti, California, New Mexico and Mexico. *The Plumed Serpent*, set in Mexico, was published in 1926. It was during his stay in Mexico that Lawrence probably came closest to his ideal way of life. At first he felt akin to its indigenous cultures and ancient religions, such those practised by the Aztecs, but by the end of his visit Lawrence realized that it was impossible to graft the alien concepts of other cultures on to the centuries-old spiritual and moral values he had inherited from the western world.

In 1925 he returned permanently to Europe. Lawrence spent most of his remaining time between Italy and France. It was during this period that he wrote his most notorious novel, *Lady Chatterley's Lover*, which was published in Italy in 1928. In 1929, some of his paintings were removed by the police from an exhibition in London for being too explicit, while in the same year the typescript of *Pansies* was seized by Customs for similar reasons.

Lawrence died at the age of forty-four in Vence in the South of France on 2 March 1930. He was a man who loved life and gave his wholehearted energy to it.

Lawrence's life and all his work reveal a disgust for the rigid ideas and values of Victorian and Edwardian England. He perceived the society he was brought up in as class-ridden and a sham, and felt that sexual and social attitudes to male and female roles inhibited human relationships and restricted the natural, passionate development of society. As far as he was concerned, even established Christianity, with its emphasis on guilt and prohibition, held back the spiritual exploration of human beings.

Lawrence also rebelled against conventional forms of the novel and poetry. In this he was not alone. Writers such as Virginia Woolf in England, James Joyce (who was Irish and wrote in English) and Marcel Proust, both living in France, and William Faulkner, working in the USA, were experimenting with how to write down the thoughts of their characters. Such techniques, often influenced by Freud's investigations of the unconscious mind, known as psychoanalysis, led to 'stream of consciousness' methods of writing. Lawrence's own novels are concerned with the individual and are often very autobiographical, but they are less experimental in their style than those of many of his so-called 'Modernist' contemporaries.

Lawrence's poetry

Lawrence's poetry can be divided into roughly five phases. The **first phase** represents Lawrence's earlier poems, in *Love Poems, Amores* and *New Poems*. In his earliest poems Lawrence wrote within the poetic conventions and style of his time.

The **second phase** is represented by the poems in the cycle *Look! We Have Come Through!*, which explore the emotions that unite or divide men and women and in particular the stresses and strains of his elopement and early years with Frieda. *Loggerheads* (see page 59) hints at the turbulence of their unconventional relationship. Other poems, such as *A Youth Mowing* or *A Doe at Evening* (see page 53), describe inner states of mind. Many of the poems in this collection resemble notebook fragments or diary entries. In these poems Lawrence begins to experiment with form and the use of rhythm to enhance emotion. Surprisingly, although placed in the 'Unrhyming' volume of the *Collected Poems*, many are written in a formal way and do rhyme, but Lawrence placed them in the second half of his collection to show that they came from a time in his life when he had gained more sexual, social and emotional maturity.

The **third phase**, *Birds, Beasts and Flowers*, is a sequence of poems divided into sections. Here, Lawrence seems to establish a relationship with the natural world which is both more intimate and more sympathetic than seen in his poems about people. He recognizes the essential life-force in creatures and the beautiful energy of nature. The poems were composed during Lawrence's travels in Europe, Ceylon (Sri Lanka) Australia, Tahiti, California, New Mexico and Mexico. These poems show him searching for alternatives and yearning for the simple creative values of Nature; along with *Pansies* and his last poems, they convey a developing and idiosyncratic view of the world. The poet was feeling greatly unsettled by the failure, as he saw it, of Europeans to tackle the ills of the modern world. *Mosquito* (see page 71) questions the role of man and explores the processes that arouse, sustain and regulate human behaviour.

Lawrence's **fourth phase** is again a time of experiment. *Pansies* contains poems written after Lawrence returned to Europe. They are often acerbic, and in poems such as *The Optimist* and *Censors* there is a sense of cynicism and disappointment about the way modern humans perceive the physical and spiritual world. In his introduction to the collection Lawrence wrote: 'Each little piece is a thought...with its own blood of emotion and instinct running in it like the fire in a fire-opal...At least, they do not pretend to be half-baked lyrics of melodies.'

The **final phase** consists of Lawrence's *Last Poems*, which were composed as the poet turned to confront his own approaching death and consider questions of mortality through the myths of the peoples and gods of the Mediterranean. The two most famous poems from this time are *Bavarian Gentians* and *The Ship of Death* (see pages 133 and 143). Both contemplate death and resurrection. The other poems from this period are connected to these two by the use of similar symbolism and themes.

Lawrence's style and techniques

From early on in his writing Lawrence experimented with different poetic forms, styles and subjects. Sometimes his work is deeply serious, or respectful of those aspects of life he held in high regard, while at other times his work is ironic or mocking.

There has been a tendency to brush Lawrence's poems aside as 'clumsy vessels' rather than stressing the merits of his unorthodox style. Lawrence's best poems have a fluid and suggestive character.

The Demon

In his introduction to the *Collected Poems* Lawrence describes his early poems as 'struggling to say something which it takes a man twenty years to be able to say...A young man is afraid of his demon and puts his hand over the demon's mouth sometimes and speaks for him. And the things a young man says are rarely poetry'. This demon, a spirit of creativity, was the power-house of his early inspiration. Gradually, Lawrence was able to achieve greater technical expertise and then finally reject the shackles of traditional poetic forms and so find styles that would allow his demon – that is his spirit, his spontaneous feelings to emerge.

Rhyming or Unrhyming Poetry and Free Verse

Lawrence's poetry has often been criticized for its lack of form. However, Lawrence believed that poetic form could be developed if verse became more casual and conversational. In order to understand form in Lawrence's poetry you need to understand the difference between verse in metre where lines of poetry repeat regular patterns of stressed and unstressed syllables and free verse which does not use regular, repeated patterns. (See Activities, *Dog Tired*, on page 1 for help with identifying stressed and unstressed syllables.)

Many Victorian and Edwardian poets used regular patterns of rhythm and rhyme. In Lawrence's early poems he writes within such patterns. He often does so to good effect, for example *Piano* shows a competent use of traditional poetic form. The rhyme-scheme employed here might be cumbersome and affected, but the resulting stress on the rhyme-words helps a reading of the poem.

In his later poems Lawrence moves into free verse. Free verse, according to Lawrence, 'is, or should be, direct utterance from the instant, whole man'. His free verse reveals a fluidity and a musical use of sounds and words. In his introduction to a collection called *New Poems*, Lawrence explained his thinking. He saw two main kinds of poetry: the first is the poem that has a finality and a sense of completion conveyed in 'the perfect symmetry, the rhythm which returns upon itself like a dance where the hands link and loosen for the supreme moment of the end...'; the second type of poem is never finished, it is free verse, which is not limited by the conditions of the standard forms of verse.

When looking at Lawrence's use of free verse the reader must decide if all his experiments in form and language give a clear insight into his world and at the same time inspire a personal response. Successful free verse is expressive, can be used to define meaning, and should not appear accidental.

Rewriting

Many of Lawrence's poems first appeared in literary and poetry magazines. Lawrence often altered his poems or their titles and created different published versions. There are numerous examples of Lawrence's need to redraft his work, changing phrases or individual words and so altering its meaning. This approach to his writing belies the frequent accusation that Lawrence was not a careful or craftsmanlike poet. His attitude emphasizes his view that words, both in poetry and prose, are living things, and a means to an end rather than an end in themselves.

Rhythm and the Emotional Mind

In a letter to his friend, Edward Marsh, dated 18 August 1913, Lawrence explained that 'my rhythms fit my mood pretty well, in the verse. And if the mood is out of joint, the rhythm often is. I have always tried to get an emotion out in its own course, without altering it'. The poems in *Look! We Have Come Through!* are excellent examples of his early attempts to enhance emotion by the use of rhythm.

In *Pansies* Lawrence began to experiment once again with a new kind of expression of emotion and thought. Most of these poems are snatches of instant expression. Poems such as *Spray* and *Sea-Weed* (see pages 113, 115) are excellent examples of this spontaneity. They, like the other *Pansies*, demonstrate his view that thoughts were different from opinions and were part of an impulsive process of exploration. He was convinced that thought was intuitive and so he devised the notion of the 'Emotional Mind', in which emotion and thinking combine through a commotion of passion and pain leading on to a decision or belief. Many of the last poems reveal this powerful transformation.

Diction, Imagery and Symbolism

Many of Lawrence's best poems are characterized by careful diction and exploration through word-painting. He often seems to have a painter's eye when describing a scene. In *End of Another Home Holiday* (see page 21), he infuses seemingly homely images of village houses, the church, a young cow and a bird with sinister and uneasy qualities, which reveal the state of his thoughts. These 'collected images' are less straightforward than similes or metaphors, but in a very striking way they help the reader to comprehend the poet's emotions and thoughts.

Lawrence also used vernacular or colloquial speech, most often his childhood local dialect. In *A Youth Mowing* (see page 53), the vernacular functions on two levels. It emphasizes the rural setting and also conveys Lawrence's empathy with the mower, then his sympathy for the young man's plight.

Lawrence's poetry generally displays mental and visual clarity. He often reinforces his meaning by extending his imagery. In *Snap-Dragon*, for example, Lawrence combines the natural and the human worlds by repeating images and revealing layers of symbolism. In stanza 1, 'The mellow sunlight stood as in a cup', but by stanza 6 the cup has become 'My Grail, a brown bowl twined. With swollen veins that met in the wrist' as the girl, the object of his desire, squeezes the flower. The colour brown recurs in the following stanzas until the girl, a 'settling bird' in stanza 3, evolves into the 'brown bird' of stanzas 12 and 13 where the image symbolizes passion.

In the internal dialogue of *Snake*, Lawrence again uses imagery and symbolism to reveal two levels of experience. The first is the mysterious, dark but natural world of the golden snake, and the second the perverse voice of the 'accursed human education' which exposes the narrator's cowardice. **Repetition** is Lawrence's most consistent stylistic technique. So in stanza 5, the snake 'flickered his two-forked tongue from his lips' but in stanza 12 after drinking, the snake 'flickered his tongue like a forked night on the air', where 'night' becomes part of the magical and dark natural forces symbolized by the snake.

In the last poems, imagery alluding to events, personalities and places from Mediterranean myth all take on symbolic resonance. In *Bavarian Gentians* the narrator's observation of the dark flowers is woven into the myth of Persephone. In *The Ship of Death* the metaphor of the vessel carrying the soul represents a coming to terms with death.

Lawrence's Influences

Lawrence's sense of the beauty and power in Nature, particularly in *Birds, Beasts and Flowers*, the mystery of all living things and the search for the human spirit or 'soul', has been compared with the English Romantic movement and poets such as Blake, Coleridge and Wordsworth. Lawrence was also an admirer of Hardy's novels and poetry.

Developing poets are often influenced by earlier mentors and Lawrence acknowledged that it was through reading Walt Whitman, the nineteenth-century American poet, that he discovered his own approach to poetry and style. Lawrence liked Whitman's personal interpretation of life and his rejection of the rather narrow attitudes and values of nineteenth-century society. Whitman, like Lawrence, often antagonized the public because of his outspoken views on sexuality. With his rhetoric and voice Whitman pioneered a style of free verse that emphasized the meaning through the natural flow of the lines. In the poem *Song of Myself* published in 1855, his style, subject-matter and tone foreshadow Lawrence's experiments in poetic form.

By the time Lawrence was living with Frieda in Europe and writing the poems in *Look! We Have Come Through!*, he had begun to reject Whitman.

Lawrence's ideas and themes

Love, the Psyche and Sex

Lawrence's concern with the unconscious side of human nature reflects his own beliefs and his interest in the research of Freud into psychology. He was preoccupied with human motivation and the psyche – the human mind or soul. Sex was the great motivator and source of confrontation between human beings, which he saw as a source of renewal and the way to adjust the relationships between men and women.

Love in Lawrence's early poems is expressed as the possessive maternal love of his mother or as naive sexual love. *Virgin Youth* is full of a young man's need for sexual expression. The hold of his mother is still evident in *Piano* (see page 49). The interaction between physical love and natural beauty is made plain in the semi-phallic symbol of the flower in *Snap-Dragon* (see page 39). Lawrence felt that the sparks of these differ-

ent types of love between men and women had been dulled by twenti-
eth-century life. In the psychologically revealing poem *A Youth Mowing*,
Lawrence again suggests this potential conflict. The poem *Intimates* is
blunt in its exposé of self-love, but also hints at his own relationship with
Frieda.

Philosophy, Religion and the Mechanization of Man

Lawrence wrote that it was the industrial squalor of England and
Europe 'that betrayed the spirit of man in the nineteenth and early twen-
tieth centuries'. He felt that this 'ugliness and dehumanization killed the
intuitive faculties' and the more natural aspects of 'man'. He resented
what he saw as the destruction of our ability to respond to the beauty of
Nature and the loveliness of all human beings. Lawrence was frustrated
that humans could not see the spiritual deprivation they had brought
upon themselves. The poem *People* from *Look! We Have Come Through!*
portrays the ghost-like existence of a mass of passing people.

Lawrence's travels around the world were part of his search for a way
of understanding life and its purpose. For example, in the poems of
Birds, Beasts and Flowers he finds the balance between what he saw as the
exhaustion and spiritual bankruptcy of Western society and the per-
petually renewable force of Nature.

Death and Religion

To Lawrence an unknown 'life-force' was the origin of all things.
Despite his contempt for established religion, his own Congregational
upbringing and his knowledge of the Bible informed his language and
imagery. The major theme of the last poems of Lawrence is his own
struggle to come to terms with death. He felt that many of the philoso-
phies of the modern world, including religion, were moribund. The title
of *Death is Not Evil, Evil is Mechanical* (see page 141) aptly expresses his
feelings about the industrialized western world, but it is in poems such
as *The Greeks are Coming* and *The Argonauts* that he ironically juxtaposes
the past and the present and so reveals his vision of the future and death.
Bavarian Gentians and *The Ship of Death* bring Lawrence's exploration of
death to a conclusion. The gentians act as a torch guiding Lawrence into
mythological realms and down to death. *The Ship of Death* emphasizes
the positive creative aspect of death, and in section seven the small ship
becomes an 'ark of faith' for the 'fragile soul'. By the end of the poem a

resurrection of some kind has occurred that has more to do with the cycle of Nature than with any supernatural power.

Chaos

Linked to Lawrence's ideas on the positive attributes of conflict was his view that poets can offer an insight into the chaos of life, and that this disorder is a source of renewal. In his 1928 essay *Chaos in Poetry* Lawrence expressed this hope:

Man fixes some wonderful erection of his own between himself and the wild chaos, and gradually goes bleached and stifled under his parasol. Then comes the poet, enemy of convention, and makes a slit in the umbrella; and lo! the glimpse of chaos is a vision, a window to the sun.

In *Tortoise Family Connections* (see page 87) he uses the struggle of the tiny baby tortoise as a metaphor for the process of birth, life and death. By the end of the poem the courageous tortoise's battle is likened to Adam's existence in the Garden of Eden, and the last image is of the creature eating arrogantly and unconcerned while surrounded by the chaos of life.

EXPLORATIONS AND ESSAYS

The activities and tasks in this section are designed to explore in detail specific aspects of selected poems. They should be regarded as a springboard to discussion, research, evaluation, personal response and writing. Most can either be done individually or tackled as groupwork. The writing tasks at the end of sections can be used for shorter written pieces or essays.

From *Love Poems* and *Amores*

This section contains a variety of activities, each offering a different way to approach a poem.

Pace and Rhythm: *Dog-Tired*

Scanning a poem – marking out the stressed and unstressed syllables – can help you analyze its pace. Although much of Lawrence's early poetry does not have a rigid structure, it does have some of the features of earlier, more formal poetry. It is important to recognize some of these repeated patterns so you can see how Lawrence adapts them and later rejects them in favour of free verse. In this poem the first stanza has been scanned for you. Try marking out the metre for the rest of the poem and see if there is any pattern.

```
 ˘    /    ˘    /    ˘   ˘   /
If she would come to me here
   /    ˘    /   ˘    /
  Now the sunken swaths
   ˘    / ˘   /
  Are glitter paths
 ˘  ˘   /    ˘  ˘    /   ˘    ˘   /
To the sun, and the swallows cut clear
 / ˘  ˘   / ˘   /   ˘ ˘   /    ˘  ˘    /
Into the setting sun! if she came to me here!
```

Discussion: *Monologue of a Mother*

1 Discuss the associations created by Lawrence's use of harsh animal imagery to express the bond between mother and son.

2 In the poem, the mother seems to be heavily influenced by three

figures in her life. Select one phrase or line to express her sense of dependency on each person.

Compare your choices with others in your group. Have you chosen the same or different lines and phrases? Why?

Comparing Poems: *Last Lesson of the Afternoon* and *A Snowy Day in School*

1 Mark out the way the rhyme scheme alters through *Last Lesson of the Afternoon*. What might the more regular pattern in the last two stanzas suggest about the poet's frame of mind? How does the poet show his changing attitude in the middle stanza of this poem?

2 Both poems use colloquial phrases. In *Last Lesson of the Afternoon* we find 'it is all my aunt' and in *A Snowy Day in School* Lawrence uses '...I must look them an answer back'. What is their purpose and how effective are they?

3 Compare how the poet explores similar sentiments in both of these school poems. Where does he reveal the lowest ebb of futility and strongest sense of the future?

Writing

The poet W.H. Auden wrote of Lawrence's early poems:

All too often in his early poems, even the best ones, [Lawrence] is content to versify his thought; there is no essential relationship between what he is saying and the formal structure he imposes upon it.

How relevant is this comment?

Comparing Poems: *Sorrow* and *Brooding Grief*

Summarize your thoughts on these two poems by writing down some of your own words to describe the feelings in them. Despite the sadness and anticipation of the forthcoming loss in his mind, do you think that in these poems Lawrence is successful in his attempt to avoid a sentimental or 'slushy' view of his life with his mother?

Close study: *Piano*

1 Scan the poem carefully and see if you can establish a regular pattern. How does the metre guide the reader to the significant phrases and images? Notice how the rhythm of a line flows over as the sentence

continues. This enjambment and rhythmic stress emphasizes the meaning.

From *Look! We Have Come Through!*

Tracing Themes

The notes below will help you to compare the themes and imagery of the poems in *Look! We Have Come Through!* You may find it useful to set your notes out as a table. For each comment you make about a poem write down the words and images you need to back up your point.

Compare:

Settings

How does Lawrence use the setting of the poem to reflect the state of mind of the poet or the state of the relationships described in the poem? Does he use similar techniques in different poems?

Views of women

How are women portrayed in these poems? What is the poet's attitude to them? Is he afraid of them? Does his attitude change throughout the poems?

People

Lawrence has been criticized for viewing some of the people in these poems (the youth mowing, the Italians) from an arrogant viewpoint. Do you agree? Are there similarities in the poems?

It could be argued that the poems are not about people at all but about the poet's own anxieties and attitudes. If so, does that make Lawrence's descriptions of the people arrogant?

Look! We Have Come Through!

The title of this section suggests a note of hope and faith in human resilience. How far is that reflected in the poems?

Writing

In his foreword to *Look! We Have Come Through!* Lawrence says:

> These poems should not be considered separately, as so many single pieces. They are intended as an essential story, or history, or confession, unfolding one from the other in organic development, the whole

revealing the intrinsic experience of man during the crisis of man-
hood, when he marries and comes into himself.

Judging from the selection here, to what extent do you feel *Look! We Have
Come Through!* reveals this 'intrinsic experience of man'?

From *Birds, Beasts and Flowers*

The activities in this section provide guidelines to help you to study
individual poems closely. Through looking at individual poems you
will develop an overall picture of Lawrence's view of the relationship
between men and women and the natural environment.

Mosquito

1 a) Make a list of quotations to show Lawrence's view of the mos-
quito's character. Does his attitude to the insect change through the
poem? (If you are working in groups, compare your quotations.) Is it
possible to divide the poem into sections as the poet's views change?

b) How does the form of free verse and the length of the stanzas used
emphasize Lawrence's train of thought and changing reaction to the
mosquito?

3 Consider the effect of Lawrence's use of 'I' and 'you' in the interplay
between the observer and the observed. What does the contrast between
the man and the insect suggest about the relationship between 'man'
and Nature?

4 Search out the repetition of words and phrases in the poem. What
effect does this technique have?

Close Study: *Snake*

1 In the first five irregular stanzas, what is the effect of the rise and fall
of the sounds in the lines (known as cadence)?

2 Identify the repetition and echoes in the description of the snake and
the earth.

3 Outline the debate the poet conducts around his contrasting views of
the snake.

4 Look at the poem from stanza eleven. What exactly do you think the
poet is afraid of?

5 In groups, prepare a reading of the poem. Choose different voices to read different views of the snake. Compare your reading with others.

6 Re-read *Snake* and choose five representative lines that seem to you to contain the 'essence' of the poem.

7 Explain what you feel the poet means in the last stanza.

Tortoise Family Connections

1 Consider how this poem compares with other poems in *Birds, Beasts and Flowers* in its attempt to understand the process of becoming, living and dying.

2 Note down the words and phrases that combine the description of nature with the comic characteristics of the baby tortoise. How does Lawrence link these physical observations with the ideas of birth, life and death in the poem?

Humming-Bird

Humming-Bird is an excellent example of Lawrence's later use of non-standard patterns of metre and rhyme

Read the poem aloud. How does Lawrence vary the pace and so speed up or slow the momentum of the poem? What effect does this have?

Eagle in New Mexico

1 Read the poem aloud and examine how Lawrence creates the force and flow of danger in the poem. Work out how the repeated images help to bring the poem together.

2 The short story *The Woman Who Rode Away* contains some of the same themes as this poem. Read it for comparison purposes. What are the common themes?

The Blue Jay

Much of Lawrence's poetry has a strong narrative element, and free verse can often seem like prose. Rewrite this poem as prose. Does it work? Does the way Lawrence has set out the poem help to guide the reader around the ideas? What do the italics add to the message in the poem?

Kangaroo

1 Make a list of the words and phrases Lawrence uses to describe the 'essence' of the animal.

2 In this poem Lawrence attributes human characteristics to the kangaroo. Why is the creature represented as so strongly female and maternal?

3 Note down the phrases which suggest that the kangaroo encapsulates and symbolizes the 'otherness' of Australia.

Tracing Lawrence's thought

Many of the poems in this section express a sympathy for living things and insight into the relationship between what Lawrence might call 'man' and the mystery of nature. Some poems also explore the huge gulf which Lawrence sees between modern, urban people and the natural environment. This exploration of the changing bond between humans and the physical universe is a major theme running through his poetry and other writing.

Trace Lawrence's view of the birds, beasts and flowers and his perception of men's and women's relationships with them throughout the poems in this section. Are Lawrence's views consistent, or does he contradict himself within and between poems? Can you see a consistent train of thought emerging?

Writing

1 Using this selection from *Birds, Beasts and Flowers*, assess the extent of Lawrence's disquiet about the failure of the human race to take a reasonable and appropriate place in the natural and physical world. How does he show the strength and dignity of Nature?

2 Lawrence wrote in a letter in 1919: 'I am going away from the land and the nation of my soul as well as of mere domicile.' What great spiritual journey is chronicled by the poems of *Birds, Beasts and Flowers*?

From *Pansies* and *More Pansies*

The activities in this section are explorations of individual poems.

Beyond the Rockies

1 Brainstorm any modern or older associations connected with the new moon. What might the new moon imply in this poem, and what threads might be cut as the moon progresses through its cycle?

2 Lawrence's idea that primitive cultures are superior to those of the modern world, generally known as primitivism, is evident in the message of this poem. What phrases in this poem imply that the ancient Mexicans had knowledge of life that we 'in the west' no longer have?

Elephants in the Circus and *The Performing Elephants*

These are taken from a group of poems about circus elephants.

1 Jot down the key images in the first poem. How are they associated with the imagery in the second?

2 Explain the implicit comparisons the poet is making between the creatures and the children in the audience.

3 The subject of the poem is the elephant but what general Lawrentian theme does this poem hint at?

What is He?

This poem is set out like a conversation. On one level the poet is writing about people in general, but who might Lawrence be alluding to in a religious sense? Discuss what you think is the central message of the poem.

Poverty

1 The so-called 'Lady' is shown to be really an old hag, and is contrasted with the natural abundance of the pine tree. Identify the images in the second part of the poem which are common to other poems in the selection.

2 Pick out one or two phrases which help to explain what Lawrence is really saying about poverty in this poem. What does he mean in the last lines when he asks for 'natural abundance'? Do you think these values are important?

Now It's Happened

1 Consider whether the connection established between the political

and literary figures really helps to reinforce Lawrence's point of view in the poem.

2 Would you consider that the use of rhyme in the poem is central to its impact, or is it incidental?

3 Paraphrase the poem, bearing in mind the cynicism of the last stanza.

Trees in the Garden

1 Select the phrases which in your opinion reveal the atmosphere before the storm. What qualities do the different trees have for Lawrence? What do the trees symbolize in this poem? Why are the trees 'strangers in the garden'?

2 Identify the tree imagery in other poems in the selection. Can you identify a symbolic use of the tree in Lawrence's poetry?

Writing

1 The *Pansies* have been criticized for being clichéd, trite and even formless. Use the poems in this selection to justify or reject the view that the writing in *Pansies* is crude and that not all of the poems qualify as verse. Consider whether the poems are too subjective to convey significant meaning to the reader.

2 How far are these poems from *Pansies* a criticism of either Christian doctrine or materialistic values, and so a celebration of the connections between humans and the organic natural world?

3 In a letter written in 1928, Lawrence wrote:

– you've got to smash money and this possessive spirit. I get more revolutionary every minute, but for life's sake. The dead materialism of Marx, Socialism and Soviets seems to me no better than what we have got. What we want is life and trust: men trusting men and making living a fine thing, not a thing to be earned.

Do the poems in this selection reflect Lawrence's heartfelt cry? If so, how?

Later Poems

The activities in this section help you to explore the complex imagery and symbolism in *Last Poems*.

The Argonauts

1 For Lawrence, the symbolism of the sun and moon is always signifi-
cant. The sun is life-giving, while the moon is often a symbol of death.
What other associations does Lawrence create with the similes of the sun
as lion and the moon as queen in *The Argonauts?* Which of the two is
more potent here?

2 Discuss how the voyage of the Argonauts and Odysseus into the
unknown parallels Lawrence's situation. Write a paragraph explaining
what you think Lawrence really has in mind in this poem.

Bavarian Gentians

1 This poem, like many of Lawrence's *Last Poems*, is visionary. Con-
sider how its repetition and cyclical style constitute an attempt to ap-
proach death through subtle modulations of symbolism and imagery.

2 The poem combines intense feeling with ingenious ideas and com-
plex imagery to carry through its theme. So the dark flower acts as an
'inverse candle' that helps to guide the soul down to the land of death.
Look at the way the imagery of darkness and death develops phrase by
phrase. Then note how the symbolism, including the mythical charac-
ters, broadens as the imagery progresses.

3 a) How far do you think the reference to the myth of Persephone and
Pluto suggests that the poet sees the possibility of some ongoing life
after death?

b) Pick out words which convey a paradoxical sense of energy in the
'dense gloom' of death.

c) How far do you think the poet sees the possibility of renewal in death?

d) The following three lines are taken from Lawrence's earlier version
of the poem:

> Give me a flower on a tall stem, and three dark flames,
> for I will go to the wedding, and be wedding-guest
> at the marriage of the living dark.

Do you find this a more positive conclusion than the ending of the later
version? Do you think the poet's attitude to death is less ambiguous
here?

Mana of the Sea

1 How does the 'mana' in this poem relate to other ideas and themes in Lawrence's poetry?

2 Discuss in what way this poem summarizes the imagery and the poet's attitude to the sea in poems in this section.

Mystic and Anaxagoras

1 In *Mystic*, Lawrence uses figurative language and imagery to describe aspects of the apple he broods over. Jot down the phrases which describe the qualities he perceives. Does he have any underlying affinity with the fruit (which is of course created by a tree and originates from the earth)? How do some of the phrases recognize the negative aspects of Nature? What does the apple represent?

2 From your reading of Lawrence's poems, suggests why being 'mystic' and 'eating' the apple with all his 'senses awake' is so important to an artist such as Lawrence, especially at this stage in his life.

3 How similar are the ideas in *Anaxagoras*?

The Ship of Death

1 Trace the references to oblivion throughout the poem.

2 In what other ways is death described or alluded to in the poem.

3 Explain what has 'bruised' the soul in section II. How else does Lawrence describe the soul

4 In your view, does the soul find a final resting place or is death a journey with no end?

All Souls' Day

1 Consider whether the regular form of this poem reveals a stability in Lawrence's thoughts as the poem progresses from his appeal to 'be careful' to 'be kind' and on to the request in the last stanza.

2 Discuss the analogy between the city and the body in the second stanza. Does it inform and widen your understanding of Lawrence's fascination with ancient cities, or is it a new concept?

Shadows

1 Consider how this poem harks back to the themes and imagery of *The*

Ship of Death. In what sense is Lawrence's interpretation of the oblivion concept in lines 1–4 different from *The Ship of Death* or any other of the *Last Poems*?

2 Despite his mention of 'God' in this poem, Lawrence was profoundly un-Christian in his attitude to death. What are the hopes he expresses at the end of the poem?

3 Read *Ode to a Nightingale* by Keats and compare his discourse on death with Lawrence's musing in this poem.

We Have Gone Too Far

1 Pick out the most important phrases or sentences in the poem and see if you can condense the meaning into a few lines.

2 Explain the many facets of the Ghosts in the poem. What do they symbolize? How might love in Lawrence's view lead people back into an understanding of life?

Writing

1 Holly Laird suggests that the *Last Poems* act as 'a vehicle for Lawrence to wrestle through his thoughts in a journey larger than any single poem could encompass'.

Explain, with examples, how many of the poems in this selection are ancillary to *The Ship of Death* and so act as satellites carrying similar meanings, themes and symbolism.

2 In the introduction to a collection of *Last Poems*, Richard Aldington referred to the *The Ship of Death* in which the 'suffering and the agony of departure are turned into music and reconciliation'. How applicable is this idea to *The Ship of Death* or any of Lawrence's last poems?

3 Explain, with references, how in *Bavarian Gentians* Lawrence explores concepts of Nature, religious beliefs and feelings about death through the detailed description of flowers.

Essay Questions

1 To what extent would you agree with the assertion that Lawrence did not really worry about poetic form?

2 Lawrence evolved a way of writing poetry that in its freedom and spontaneity allowed him to show what he called 'the palpitating moment of being and the naked self'.

Using your knowledge of the poems, say how far you agree with this statement.

3 In an essay entitled *Poetry of the Present* Lawrence wrote of Whitman's poetry 'the clue to all his utterance lies in the sheer appreciation of the instant moment, life surging itself into utterance at its very well-head'. To what extent is this statement true of his own poetry?

4 The introduction to *Pansies* (1929) also conveys to the reader Lawrence's 'philosophy of life':

For by pretending to have roots, we have trodden the earth so hard over them that they are starving and stifling below the soil. We have roots, and our roots are the sensual, instinctive and intuitive body, and it is here we need the fresh air of open consciousness.

Relate this statement to your knowledge of his poetry.

5 In his last years of illness Lawrence wrote to a friend:

The whole scheme of things is unjust and rotten and money is just a disease upon humanity. It is time there was an enormous revolution – not to install the Soviets but to give life itself a chance. What's the good of an industrial system piling up rubbish, while nobody lives?

How does Lawrence's poetry reflect this philosophy?

W R I T I N G   A N   E S S A Y
A B O U T   P O E T R Y

Your own personal response to a poet and his or her work is of major importance when writing an essay on poetry, either as part of your course or as an examination question. However, this personal response needs to be based on a solid concept of how poetry works, so you must clearly show that you understand the methods the poet uses to convey the message and ideas of the poem to the reader. In most cases, unless it is relevant to your answer, you should not pad out your essay with biographical or background material.

Planning

Look carefully at the wording of the question. Underline the important words and ideas. Make sure you apply your mind to these key elements of the question and then explore them in the essay.

Bring all your knowledge of, and opinions on, a poet and his or her poetry to this first stage of writing. Brainstorm your ideas and always combine these thoughts in a plan that shows the development and intention of your answer. Your plan must outline the structure of your essay. In exam conditions, the plan and the direction of your comments may take you only a few minutes and should be little more than a way of laying out your ideas in order. However the plan must be an outline of how and where you are going to link your evidence to the opinions and concepts of the essay. Reject any ideas which are not relevant at the planning stage. Remember that your plan should be arranged around your ideas and not the chronological order of a poem or a poet's work, or your essay will be weakened.

Writing

Your introduction must implicitly or, if you wish, explicitly make the teacher or examiner realize that you understand the question.

Don't spend a lot of time spotting, defining and examining poetic techniques and form. If you do identify these features, then you must be sure of the poetic terms and be able to show why they are significant in the verse and to the poet's attempts to create a 'meaning' and a message.

Make absolutely sure that your answer is clear and that it tackles the issues in the question precisely. Try to offer points for discussion and apply your knowledge in an interesting way. Don't go ahead and disregard what the question asks you to write about, then write the essay you want to write. Don't waffle, don't write too elaborately or use terms vaguely; at the same time, don't be too heavy-handed with your views. Strive to put your opinions directly and accurately.

In exam conditions be aware of the time, and if you are running out of your allotted span then make sure that you put down your most important ideas in the minutes left. Try to leave a few minutes to revise and proof-read your script. Be sure that the points you have made make sense and are well supported by evidence. Don't try to introduce new ideas as you write unless they are essential to your essay. Often these extra thoughts can distract you from the logic of your argument. If it is essential, then refer back to your plan and slot the idea into the right part of the essay.

Bring your ideas together at the end of the essay. Make sure that you have put your views clearly and, if necessary, express the main thrust of your views or argument again.

Quotations

Quotations are a vital source of evidence for the viewpoints and ideas you express in your essay. Try not to misquote and remember that when using extracts of more than a few words you should place them separately outside your text as they would be laid out in the poem.

If you follow the advice here you will produce a clear, relevant and logical essay. Try to spend time reading and listening to the comments of your teacher and make your own notes on your work for revision purposes.

A NOTE FROM A CHIEF EXAMINER

Your examination script is the medium through which you communicate with your examiner. As a student, you will have studied what writers say and how they say it; your examiner will assess what *you* say and how you say it. This is the simple process through which your knowledge and understanding of the texts you have studied is converted into your examination result.

The questions which you will find on your examination paper have been designed to enable you to display your ability to engage in short, highly concentrated explorations of particular aspects of the texts which you have studied. There is no intention to trick you into making mistakes, rather to enable you to demonstrate to your examiner your knowledge and understanding. Questions take a variety of forms. For a poetry text, you may be asked to concentrate on one poem, or a particular group of them, and provide detailed examination of some features of the writing. You may be asked to range widely throughout a poet's work, exploring specified aspects of his or her style and themes. You may be asked to provide a considered personal reaction to a critical evaluation of the poet's work.

Whatever the question, you are, ultimately, being asked to explore what and how, content and style. Equally, you are being asked for a personal response. You are communicating to your examiner your own understanding of the text, and your reactions to it, based on the studies you have undertaken.

All of this may seem very simple, if not self-evident, but it is worthwhile to devote some time to thinking about what an examination is, and how it works. By doing so, you will understand why it is so important that you should prepare yourself for your examination in two principal ways: first, by thorough, thoughtful and analytical textual study, making your own well-informed evaluation of the work of a particular writer, considering what he or she is conveying to you, how this is done, how you react, and what has made you respond in that way; then, by practising the writing skills which you will need to convey all these things to your examiner.

When assessing your script and awarding marks, examiners are working to guidelines which instruct them to look for a variety of different qualities in an essay.

These are some of the things which an examiner will consider.

- How well has the candidate understood the essay question and the given task? Is the argument, and the material used to support it, entirely relevant?

- Is quotation used aptly, and textual reference employed skillfully in discussion?

- Is the candidate aware of how and why the writer has crafted material in a particular way?

- Is there evidence of engagement with the text, close analytical reading, and awareness of subtleties in interpretation?

- Does the candidate have the necessary vocabulary, both general and critical, to express his or her understanding lucidly? Are technical terms integrated into discussion?

- Can the candidate provide an interesting, clearly expressed and structured line of argument, which fully displays a well-informed personal response?

From these points, you should be able to see the kind of approach to examination questions which you should avoid. Re-hashed notes, second-hand opinion, unsupported assertion and arid copies of marginal jottings have no place in a good script. Don't fall into the trap of reproducing a pre-planned essay. Undoubtedly you will find (if your preparation has been thorough) that you are drawing on ideas which you have already explored in other essays, but all material used must be properly adapted to the task you are given. Don't take a narrative approach; paraphrase cannot replace analysis. Do not, under any circumstances, copy out chunks of introduction or critical notes from your text in an open book examination. Nor do you need to quote at excessive length; your examiner knows the text.

It is inevitable that, when writing in examination conditions, you will only use quite a small amount of the material you have studied in order to answer a particular question. Don't feel that what you are not using has been wasted. It hasn't. All your studies will have informed the understanding you display in a succinct, well-focused answer, and will equip you to write a good essay.

Virginia Graham

SELECT BIBLIOGRAPHY

Lawrence's works

The semi-autobiographical novel, *Sons and Lovers*, is essential and complementary reading for the early poems.

Three Plays by D.H. Lawrence (Penguin, 1969) is an interesting alternative source of information and also an insight into the early life of Lawrence. The plays complement the early poems.

The Rainbow and *Women in Love*, written five years apart, tell the story of the Brangwen family and particularly the two sisters Ursula and Gudrun. Both are tragic novels which show evidence of Lawrence's interest in and feeling for the psychological theories being expounded by Freud and Jung.

The background to *The Plumed Serpent* is the clash between the primitive, old-world rituals and values of Mexican Indians and the materialism and depraved consciousness of the modern Western world.

On his return to Europe from Mexico, Lawrence found another source of ideas about life and death in the myths of the Etruscans, the pre-Roman inhabitants of northern Italy, and set them down in the travel bood *Etruscan Places*.

Mara Kalnins (ed.), *D.H. Lawrence – Selected Poems* (Everyman, 1992) has a fuller selection of poems.

Vivian de Sola Pinto and Warren Roberts (eds). *The Complete Poems of D.H. Lawrence* (Penguin, 1977).

A Glover (ed.), *The Works of D.H. Lawrence* (The Wordsworth Poetry Collection, 1994).

Criticism and biography

Philip Hobsbaum, *A Reader's Guide to D.H. Lawrence* (Thames and Hudson, 1981) has two very interesting chapters on Lawrence's poetry.

Gamini Salgado, *A Preface to Lawrence* (Longman, 1982) explains the life, works and concerns of Lawrence in more detail.

Neil Champion, *D.H. Lawrence – Life and Works* (Wayland, 1989) is a straightforward account of his life and works.